In Search

of the Lost Ones

To Julie
all the best

Rebecca A. Emrich

In Search

of the Lost Ones

*The German Soldiers of
Transylvania in the Second World
War And Their Stories*

REBECCA A. EMRICH

First Printing, 2011
For *Love of Books*
Vancouver, British Columbia

ISBN-13:
9780986600906

ISBN-10:
0986600903

For Alexandra and Bethany

One day you'll read this book and understand why.

Acknowledgements

A book such as this one cannot be written by only one person. There are many people I need to thank for their time and efforts. It was their support that made this book a reality.

Mike and Rose Emrich, so much of this book depended upon your support and to simply say thanks would not be enough.

Thanks also to John and Judy Penteker. The help you have given me is more than I can express in these pages. You were instrumental in pointing me in the right direction for interviews and books, and you spent many hours of editing to help express what life was like during a time of war. I knew I could rely on you to gracefully and consistently inform me of errors in the overall wording of the book because a simple German phrase does not translate so simply after all.

To Jane Penteker, thank you for being my editor, my sounding board and a wonderful support.

To Dr. Waldemar Scholtes, who spent time and energy in giving me primary documents on the Second World War that related to Transylvania and the Saxons of the area: You were also instrumental in correcting and improving this book. With your help, the traditions of the Saxons became more alive and more understandable to me for this book.

To Dr. Steven Harold, my many thanks for your hard work in reading, and editing. I am grateful for your time and your suggestions to improving.

To First Editing, many thanks for making this a better book and something which I am pleased to publish. Your suggestions and editing are a blessing.

To Anna, Peter, Katharina, Sofia, Stephan, Andreas, Martin, Georg, Maria, Hilda, Matilde and the countless others whom I interviewed for this book, my thanks for your time and memories. The stories you have shared mean more to me now than you will ever understand. Your stories prove that it is not the war but the people who truly matter. In this book, I will try to show that to the world.

Introduction

The Second World War destroyed more lives than any other single event in the last two centuries of world warfare. It is fair to say that if it had not ruined so much, I would not be alive, or at least I would not be where I am now. This was a defining period for the Saxon people, when many men died, and then entire families were ordered to move. The Russians moved through Romania very quickly and they sent the men and women that they captured to labour camps and many did not survive.

If you ask a Saxon person a question about what happened between 1942 and 1946, he or she will only offer general comments or will refuse outright to talk about the life they led in a land that they loved. This presented me with a challenge because many of the Saxon writings I could find are now out of date or based only on word of mouth knowledge.

The people known as the Saxons are ethnically of German origin. They lived within the borders of Transylvania, and most of them recall that it was lush, green, and fertile, and most of all it was their own land. To them, Transylvania was and still is the land where they grew up. They now pass these feelings and memories on to other people, children and grandchildren like me, who were born in new homelands. When one asks about their lives, the stories they often tell start exactly where the Saxons themselves began.

The Saxons left parts of what is now present day Germany for Transylvania in the twelfth century, and depending upon who you wish to believe, there were between 2,000 and 20,000 of them, invited by the king Geza II, to move to Transylvania increase the local population and to help defend the Kingdom of Hungary.[1] There is a bit of romanticism in the story of the Saxons, at least about their origins[2] – other people do not see that, at least not in their history – they see an industrious people who can be trusted to complete tasks in a timely manner. They did not leave from what is now Saxony, but from the Rhine regions and the Mosel regions of what was the Holy Roman Empire.

According to author Ernst Wagner and others, the number of Saxons who immigrated to the Transylvania area was never as high as the people might say. Some Saxons proclaim that their story can be found in history books, and they often suggested that to me when I asked some specific questions. When I prodded further, though, they conceded there was of course more to the story. They also want to pay homage to the professors and other learned people who have studied Saxon history and traditions. They are a humble people, and they know more about their lives, history, and traditions than they give themselves credit for.

The Saxons lived a great life. Each person accepted his or her role in that life, and it did not do to complain. A person's life path was pre-defined by gender and everyone worked for the greater good of the village. They did not dwell much on individual thoughts and dreams. The boys often grew up to be farmers, and the girls married young, raised their children and cared for the family and the house. It was a patriarchal society. Few women in the Saxon communities chose to become teachers or take up a trade. If a man chose to be a pastor or pursue some other profession, it was likely that someone else in the family had followed that path before.

Within the span of twenty years, the life they led would change. In 1919, after the conclusion of the First World War, the Paris Peace Talks awarded Transylvania to Romania. The Saxon community in the city of Alba Iulia (called Karlsburg by the German speakers) was among many of the ethnic groups who voted in favour of joining Romania. This was a possible reaction to the Hungarian attempts of Magyarization[3] after the year of 1867, when the Empire of Austria and the Kingdom of Hungary united. Many Saxons, Jews, and Hungarians ceded land to the victors of the war, the Romanians. According to the Saxons, that was when they were most heavily taxed and lost nearly everything that they had.

Again, the truth is more complex. The Romanians appropriated the land that the Saxons owned and taxed them at a higher rate than the ethnic Romanian citizens. When Transylvania was part of the Austro-Hungarian Empire they were not taxed at such a high rate as they were after the end of the First World War. The loss of land was more consequential to them, psychologically, than the high taxes. The Lutheran church once owned a lot of the fertile land as well, and the loss of this land along with parts of their personal farmsteads left many villagers with a feeling that a part of them was ripped away. Many Saxons would argue that the Golden Charter of the Transylvanian Saxons, the agreement made between them and King Geza II and extended by King Andrew II in 1224, should remain in force. It did not and this lead to the bitter feeling that they had received less than they were promised.

The Second World War began in 1939, and several territorial changes affected many of the people whose stories are told in this book. In 1940, the Second Vienna Awards transferred Northern Transylvania to Hungary, and the southern part of Transylvania remained as Romanian territory. (The First Vienna Awards, in 1938, transferred territory from Czechoslovakia to Hungary.) Most of the men in the following stories would live in Hungary until the end of the war. This was noteworthy because Hungary was the only Axis country to gain territory by peaceful means. The Axis included Greater Germany (which was an amalgamation of Germany and Austria) and Italy, as well as Hungary and for a time, Romania.

However, this did not mean that the Saxons would have lands returned or find more power in Hungary. Rather, it resulted in a migration of ethnic populations between Southern Transylvania and Northern Transylvania, mostly of Romanians leaving for the South and the Hungarians leaving for the Northern part of Transylvania[4]. According to many Saxon sources, Wagner included, the Saxons in both the north and the south did not leave their homes or land until the mandatory evacuation of Northern Transylvania in 1944. The people in Northern Transylvania resented being cut off from Hermannstadt (Sibiu), the religious and cultural centre for the Saxons[5].

Many men and women told me that they were still taxed and this created hardships of a different sort as the war drew closer to them. Troops were retreating from the combined armies in the East and entire villages evacuated their people to safe places away from the fighting, most people understood that the life they lead was changing and they did not know what they would face. Some villages were not evacuated quickly enough and the people were forced back to their homes by advancing Russian soldiers.

After 1941, changes happened rapidly and families began to lose men because of the great push into Russia by Germany and its allies. Although World War II began in 1939 with the invasion of Poland, the quick victory in France meant that few Saxon soldiers needed to take part in that invasion or the subsequent occupation of Western Europe. That changed when Germany declared war on Russia (The Union of Soviet Socialist Republics) in 1941.

In September 1944, the Northern Saxons were ordered to evacuate the land they owned by the commander of the German forces in Northern Transylvania, General Arthur Phelps. The Soviet Red Army was moving into the Hungarian zone, and since Romania was now allied with Russia and the Southern Saxons were told to remain within the Romanian zone of Transylvania. From there, many of them were deported to labour camps in the Soviet Union because of their German heritage.

The Saxons from the north who left for Germany also faced hard times once they arrived in their new homeland. They found that there was little land available for farming because many people came into the much smaller territory of Germany after the war ended. Many Saxons later immigrated to Canada and the United States. In this book, they have shared these memories, after moving to faraway lands in search of something better or something that they had lost because of their German ethnic ties.

Many of the people I interviewed told me that their memories of some of the events in their lives are starting to fail, and there are some things that they have deliberately chosen to forget. These were not good times, and people suffered. When I spoke with them, I found that if I rephrased my questions once or twice I could sometimes get a bit more information, but the tone was the same; the pain ran deep with many of these people. They were Germans, but not Germans – and they would soon become the enemy.

I have changed some of the first names of these men and women because many of them have very common names. Among the men, Johann is the most commonly used name in many Saxon villages, followed closely by Michael, Peter and Georg. Maria, Anna, Rosina, Sophia are the most common names for women. To limit confusion, each person had a Saxon "Dorfname" or village nickname that their friends and families used to identify them. For the sake of clarity, I have chosen to replace these common first names with ones that were authentic to each village, but not used as often. In addition to the books referenced in the citations, I have extended the bibliography to help the reader further understand the events mentioned by the men and women I interviewed for this book.

Forever Loved...
Gone Too Soon

The sniper crouches in his snow-covered tree, waiting. He knows that soon a train containing more enemy targets will arrive. He covers his mouth against the bitter cold and prepares. His requirements: white camouflage and a perfect target, one that will strike panic in the others. No one will see him. He needs to make certain there is no chance of escape. He grins when he hears the distant sound of the train and sees the plume of smoke rising up against the land. His targets are coming. They are never human – to consider the targets as such would be harmful to his duty to his country. His only job is to kill, and he lost count of the dead many years ago.

The train slows to a halt and with the heat from the steam and the grinding of the wheels the cold and silence is broken. The train door rattles open. Out of the train jumps the first target, and the sniper takes careful aim, and as he pulls the trigger, the sniper sees the face of the man, his gentle brown eyes darting around in the light as if he has seen the sniper... then the target... the man... falls, unmoving, to the ground.

Anna loves Johann with all her heart. She will love him until the day she dies. She is never his widow, always his wife. He is the handsome man she adored, and his quiet character was the quality that drew her to him. There was so much about him that she loved. She aches so much for his voice, his smile, and his tender words. She looks at the faded photographs on her wall, the one of the two of them on their wedding day, another of her, him and two of their children, and there is one of him alone, taken before they were married, that sits on the mantel-piece. They are little mementos of a life long past. Now, as her life draws closer to its end, she feels the need to tell their story. His grandchildren deserve to know about him. They do not have anything. Neither do his great-grandchildren, and although she fears they will not know about her, they must know about him. She is the bearer of that trust; his letters are long since lost, though she kept them as long as she could. She gazes into the distance, willing time to stop, to give her the chance to tell the story of his life... their life, their love, to the people who need to learn and carry on his memory. The war sent him far away – so far from his beloved home in the rolling mountains of Transylvania, and far from her.

January 1910 was a time of cold death, but it also marked the beginning a new life. Johann's birth into a farming family in the small village of Heidendorf with the aid of a midwife was uneventful. At the tender age of four weeks old, his parents baptized him in the imposing white church at the center of the village. His childhood was a mix of games and work. This would change with the beginning of World War I, when his father and other men left the village to do something that his mother explained to him was a duty to the Austro-Hungarian Empire. His mother and the other women of Heidendorf spent many tearful nights waiting for news of victory or defeat, and the fate of the men they loved. Johann would later tell Anna that some of those men never returned, and the ones who did were not the same as they had been when they left.

The Transylvania he could recall was changing: the govern-ment took more land away from the Saxons like him and gave it to the Romanian people; it was 1919 and Johann was now a Romanian citizen with less farmland and more taxes. He told his brother-in-law, Peter, that he had learned this work-ing in the fields. The men of the village now faced less work and more worry. When he was five, Johann learned first-hand about the destructive forces of discrimination and war, and they had a profound impact on him. This was happening all over the world, not just in Transylvania, but it was the personal impact on him and his father that he would explain to his family later on.

He was a German, a person who had lost the war, and the victors, the Romanian people, exacted their price. They took the land from Johann's father and his church and used it for their own, and they raised taxes that the Germans and the other non-Romanians needed to pay. Now there was less land and less money for many people. His new understanding of the "Justice for the Defeated," as he later referred to it, caused him to become less boisterous and more thoughtful.

As he grew older, people began to respect him as an introspective thinker. His brother-in-law Peter remembers that people listened carefully and valued what Johann had to say because they understood that he had spent considerable time contemplating his words before he spoke. The church was a great passion in his life, and his faith grew stronger after his confirmation at the age of thirteen. After that, the rest of Heidendorf allowed Johann to share his passion for and knowledge of the Lutheran faith. After his confirmation, he joined the village boys' club, known as the "brotherhood."

This informal club would help with whatever odd jobs the church and the village needed, and the young men learned the value of organization. They also planned many dances and fellowship functions that related to the church. These events were the highlight of Johann's youth, and he would tell stories about them to his wife and brothers-in-law. They were lots of fun and they helped him to learn how people relate with one another in social settings. He valued this because sometimes he would get uncomfortable if the conversations he was involved in became too exciting. Johann did not enjoy things that turned exciting or unpredictable – he loved routine and quiet. He knew that in a few years he would have to get accustomed to a new routine – the military life.

Two years of mandatory military duty was required of all Romanian men when they turned twenty-one[6]. Shortly after he celebrated that birthday, Johann travelled by wagon to the familiar city of Bistritz with a group of other men of his age. Over the years, many of the children, Johann included, would travel with their families about six kilometres away for the city's annual fair, where the Saxon people would trade and buy anything that they needed. He later told his brother-in-law, Peter, that the city was different from how he had imagined it was, but he did not elaborate. When his family visited Bistritz, they would stay with family or other Saxon friends, so there was never a need to explore the city itself.

Bistritz was large[7], and it was home to ethnic communities of Germans, Hungarians and Romanians, and groups of colourful gypsies known as the Roma. The city boasted electricity and large textile factories and coal processing plants. Johann abhorred the fumes, the smoke and the noise from the countless factories that are the lifeblood of any ever-expanding city. In Bistritz, people lived close to one another but never seemed to care about each other, as they did in Heidendorf. He longed to return home, but he understood that his duty was to his country, Romania. After a few days, he boarded a train heading south towards the heart of the country, where he was to report for his mandatory service.

The army gave him a sense of belonging. His commanding officer came to value Johann's advice since he presented a quiet demeanour and strength – an asset to his role as a soldier. He would only speak when another person spoke to him and commanded the respect of his peers. He later told Peter that he simply followed the rules and obeyed orders, and enjoyed the outdoor marching that was a part of their daily regimen. Each day consisted of marching, lifting, and following orders. Some days they practiced shooting targets with rifles. Johann later told his wife, Anna, that this was not something he enjoyed, because he knew that if war broke out he would have two choices: die or be injured, or inflict the same on another person. This caused a dilemma for him, and he later said that this time in the army allowed him to appreciate his life as a farmer. Until he could go back to Heidendorf, though, he focused on his duty.

Johann was a perfectionist, and the army's strict schedule suited him. Although he received more money at the end of each month than he could earn as a farmer, Johann still had mixed feelings about what he might do if forced to fight in a war. He valued life, and he abhorred the idea that a soldier's primary purpose was to kill other people. He missed attending the Lutheran church services and singing the familiar hymns; the army conducted Sunday services based on the traditions of the Romanian Orthodox Church.

He was thrilled to receive letters from home, though many told him of events affecting Heidendorf in ways that made life harder for the villagers. His mother died a number of years before he had left for the army, and he was happy to hear that his father married another young woman from the village. Since Johann received money from the army, he was happy to send home what he could to help them all. He hoped to see them soon. He travelled all over Romania, but he still longed to be home with his family. The next few years passed by quickly and uneventfully. He later commented that, in the Balkans, to be a soldier in a time without conflict between nations was a blessing.

After his service was complete, he was discharged and he returned to civilian life in Heidendorf. Johann tried to make the adjustment back to farming as quickly as he could. He realized that being away for three years – he stayed longer to earn some extra money, Anna recalls – had diminished his chances of finding a suitable wife. Most of the women of his age were now married and had many children to care for; before he left, he attended many of their wedding celebrations. Johann valued the advice of many of the older men in the village. Some of these mentors of his youth now rested in the Saxon cemetery, and he

missed their comforting presence in his life. He particularly valued the wise words of his father, but soon after Johann returned
home, his father died. This saddened Johann, but he would later
tell his wife that he understood at the time that his father was
old enough to die, and he led an exemplary life. The Lutheran
church became an essential part of Johann's life again and he
attended the services every Sunday. He devoted the next two
years to the land and the church. Anna remembers how much
comfort the Bible brought Johann in his understanding of the
world. His knowledge of theology earned him a healthy measure of respect among his friends in the village, and everyone
around him valued his opinions.

In the early months of winter 1936, his life took a happy
turn. He had not yet met a woman he wanted to marry, so
he had stopped looking – and then one evening she sat down
next to him. He knew Anna, or rather he knew of her through
her father, and he decided to strike up a conversation. She was
seventeen years old, she had a similar character to his, and she
appreciated his quiet personality. After that evening, they spent
more time together, and after many weeks Johann decided to
ask her father for her hand in marriage. Her father agreed, and
Johann was delighted. Anna remembers that when they next
met, he seemed so very serious, and she worried about what
news he might be bringing – until he asked her to be his wife.
When she said 'yes,' he gave her the smile she fell in love with.

Anna remembers that the wedding ceremony was the most
wonderful event in both their lives. It took place in January[8] of
1937 and the winter was harsh, but this meant that they were
able to spend more time with each other. They spent many
evenings together and visiting with Johann's stepmother. Johann
enjoyed reading and conversation, and this was how Johann and
Anna grew to love and understand each other. He would read
aloud while she did the many household duties, and he was
always quick to praise her. When she told him that he would
soon be a father, she remembers how his happiness increased.

He hoped that the baby would be strong and healthy and might look like him. He was anxious to share with the baby all the knowledge that his father passed down to him and waited in anticipation for the blessed event. Tradition meant that girls always married and took their husband's name and would not become farmers. Their husbands would look after them and this was something he wanted to teach to his children. Perhaps for these reasons, Johann constantly referred to his unborn child as male, as "the boy," as "my son." This was second nature to him, but he was careful to tell people that a baby girl would also be a gift. Children, in his view, were a part of the reason why the Saxons and the church traditions would continue. Anna remembers he was often more concerned about her working too hard than were her own parents.

Johann was ecstatic the day a healthy daughter arrived. The baby was born early,[9] but the midwife assured him his daughter would do well. The midwife's comforting words proved correct, and the baby thrived. In the evenings, he would sing to her in a fine tenor voice. When she responded to him, it gave him great pleasure, and he often told his family how precious she was. He told his father-in-law that there would be more children and that he was not concerned that she was a girl. He waited until the day of her baptism in the Lutheran Church.

According to tradition, they named her "Anna" after her mother. After the baptismal service, he played host to the extended family. He butchered a pig for this special occasion, and his wife, his stepmother, her sisters, and mother-in-law prepared the rest of the food.

Johann's "little Anna" grew up fast, and she was soon old enough to speak and was very vocal. Johann delighted in each word she said. She would bring a smile to his face when he saw she had some of his mannerisms, especially the way she held her spoon and cup. Her gray eyes were as expressive as his were, and he told his wife that he was not bitter that they were not the same colour as his, a light brown. This annoyed Anna's mother until everyone realized that he was joking. Johann was happiest in the evenings when he was able to play with his daughter. Anna loved that Johann seemed engrossed in his games with their little girl. Johann's only wish was that his little Anna could have a sibling as a playmate. He hoped for a son who would bear the name "Johann" and the family name. Soon there was another worry: Johann did not earn enough money to support his growing family, so he and Anna decided that he should re-join the army.

The army welcomed him back, although Anna suspects that this was not only because of his previous experience. From the army's point of view, the timing was fortunate, for in 1938 rumours of a border war with Hungary were growing. Romania would soon have to fight, and the army would need every man it could find. Radio announcements informed the villagers of the talks between Germany, Great Britain, France and Italy over territory called the Sudetenland[10]. This meeting between these countries was called the Munich Agreement[11]. Anna supported Johann's decision, but she was worried that he might be walking into harm's way. War meant death and, for the defeated, the loss of land.

In 1938, Austria voted to unite with Germany to form a country called Greater Germany in what would become known as the Anschluss. The Munich Agreement, the Anschluss and the First Vienna Awards helped to avert a border crisis.

Many people, including Johann feared the repercussions. He discussed this with his father-in-law who was concerned because war could mean that his two sons, Peter and Michael, who would soon be old enough for mandatory service, faced the possibility of early recruitment if the situation worsened.

For many people, taxes were heavy. Johann made an important decision – he would increase the time he spent serving with the army. Once the spring planting was completed and he knew his family could manage, he headed back to the endless drills and marches. He missed his family and took to writing to them about his daily tasks. He also made certain that Anna read the letters to their daughter, lest she grew up not knowing her father. On weekends, he came home, often just in time to see his daughter trying to eat something she should not.

Anna remembers that the leaves from the mulberry bush were a particular favourite of her daughter's. When he first saw this, Johann dropped whatever bags he was carrying and run to stop her, but then he saw that she did this every time he came home, and when he began to suspect that she was playing games with him, he did not run as fast. Anna remembers he would always come in laughing, carrying his daughter, his bags, and whatever else he had with him. He returned to the army barracks on Sunday nights. Sometimes he could visit Heidendorf during the week for an evening because the army had built the barracks close to Heidendorf. However, being a part of the army would soon become a dangerous occupation.

In September 1939, Johann heard on the radio in the Heidendorf village hall that Germany was at war with Poland, and this new development worried him. Someone once overheard him muttering "like Belgium."[12] It took many people a while to realize what he already feared: that this war would become another war in which Britain would fight. His fears were not unfounded, and Anna remembers that days later Johann went pale when he heard that Britain and France had declared war on Germany. He was certain that Russia would join in the fighting soon as well, and the world would once again become a field of death. Anna remembers how much he prayed that there would be peace, and that he would not need to leave Heidendorf for the front lines. He told her how much he loved her and little Anna. Anna remembers it took her days to convince him that he would not die or have to kill others during the war. He would often protest that he had joined the army to make money but never to kill. He was, first and foremost, a farmer. Still, his military service was a duty that he needed to accept.

As the turmoil unfolded around them, Johann was thankful for the love of his wife and daughter. He joked that the one cross he had to bear was that his little Anna still had no siblings. He told the villagers who asked about another child that God would send one when the time was right. He built her several wooden toys, and he painted them with bright colours. Johann joked to his sisters-in-law, Katharina and Sofia, that he was never sure which little Anna liked to do more: build towers or tear them down. Anna remembers that Johann maintained an interest in the unfolding of world events, no matter how much he loved to avoid the Heidendorf hall for fear of hearing that neutral Romania was declaring war against another country.

In May of 1940, Johann heard that Germany had invaded France, and in a long discussion with his brother-in-law, Peter, he spoke passionately about the prospect of a prolonged war. There would be deaths, pain, and sorrow. Peter remembers how fanatical Johann became when he shared his memories of how long the previous war had lasted, and of the massive casualties on both sides. Peter remembers to this day the way Johann spoke, and in that moment he felt convinced that Johann was correct. As the days progressed, they heard more announcements on the radio about the defeat of France, and Johann was one of the few men in the village to disbelieve the reports at first. At night, he would argue that the French army was stronger than that and that they could not have surrendered so soon – after only seven weeks. When the village received official word of France's surrender, his demeanour changed. He was overjoyed because this meant that he would not need to choose between his family life and a military one.

Anna remembers that, during that time of that uneasy peace, there were new people that came to the village. Men from Germany – later she would learn that they were from the Nazi Party – came to many of the Saxon villages in Transylvania. There were three or four of them, they were all blond-haired and blue-eyed, and they spoke a lot about the German people. They talked about the mighty power of the Germans who were taking back that which was rightfully theirs – land and territory.

They also spent time with any of the village men whom they felt did not agree with the views of their beloved leader in Germany.

Johann was one of the many men whom they took aside to speak with in longer conversations. Ostensibly, this was to establish friendly relations between Germany and the German people who lived outside the country, but he later told Anna that they wanted information about him, his life, and his loyalty. They asked him countless questions about his life as a soldier and about the ages of his wife and daughter. They told Johann that they would speak with him again, after he had had time to think properly. Johann said to Anna that he believed that these men sought to destroy everything he valued, and possibly to kill him. She remembers telling him that he was a good man and that God would not let anything bad happen to him.

Nevertheless, he worried and brooded.

He focused on his family and continually asked his wife how she was feeling. He was overjoyed to learn that in the coming winter there would be a welcome new addition to their family. He hoped equally for a girl or a boy. He made certain that Anna was comfortable as she grew larger and that she would not need to do anything more than was necessary. Since Little Anna had been born early, he worried that the same thing might happen again, and this time with disastrous consequences. Even working in the army, he still did not have enough money to send for a doctor if there was an emergency.

He had other worries: his father-in-law, Peter, took ill[13]. Johann was convinced that the cause was the water from the well near the house, and he examined it carefully. He told his brother-in-law that if they allowed moss to grow in the well, this would affect the quality of drinking water. Then his beloved brother-in-law, Peter, also fell ill. Although he would not admit it, Anna knew that Johann felt the chances of a bountiful harvest were slight without help from his father-in-law and brother-in-law. It was with the help of Peter's younger brother Michael that they completed the backbreaking job of harvest. Michael exceeded everyone's expectations because he usually liked to joke around a lot. This was not one of these times. With the harvest in, and news that the two men whom he worried about were on the road to a full recovery, he concentrated on the upcoming birth of his second child.

While he waited for the birth of his second child, Johann found time to go with some of the other men to Bistritz to buy special items for the family. He bought jam and little gifts for the unborn child. When he returned and showed the gifts to his family, he loved to point out that little Anna loved the jam, or at least the colour of it – a bright red. He enjoyed retelling the story to everyone about his daughter's delight in the jam. He spent as much time as he could with her and his wife, and in November 1941, with the temperature dropping, his wife gave birth to their second child, a son. Johann was ecstatic. He loved looking at the new arrival, and his wife remembers that when the baby cried he would often pick him up to calm him. Although the baby was born a couple of weeks sooner than expected, he was healthy and he grew quickly. Johann was delighted to announce to people that he would name his son Johann, after him. The family tradition would continue, and he would keep his land on the hills for another generation.

Anna remembers that sometimes she would overhear him talking to his son about their land and its people. He often included his daughter. He brought her to see her younger brother and encouraged her to hold him. Johann would take her on small errands in the village, too, and promised her that in three years when she turned seven he would take her to the carnival that came to Bistritz once a year. He told his family that by the age of seven Anna would be old enough to enjoy and remember the carnival; she would also be quiet enough not to ask too many questions. Then he laughed, and Peter remembers how his mother wanted to give her son-in-law a lecture, until she realized that what he said was in jest because little Anna did not ask too many questions any more, and Johann wanted her to be able to remember the experience. In December, Johann and his family went to the church for his son's baptism. His sister-in-law, Katharina, remembers that Johann did not want the women of the family to hold his son all the time and he would often take charge of holding his baby. Since baby Johann stopped crying when his father held him, Johann seemed to feel that he had a strong argument.

He joked that the baby was growing so quickly that he would need his dress clothes shortened soon, he would walk before he was a year old, and that he would grow to be very tall. It was traditional, Anna pointed out to him, that boys would not have the dress shorted until they were a year old, and then they would start wearing pants. Johann was not too pleased that his son wore frilly dress-like clothes, but when Anna told him that all babies wore them, he reluctantly allowed it. In early 1942 the family went to have photos taken, and Johann refused to let his son be dressed in a "girl's outfit," as he called it, for the occasion. In that photograph, baby Johann wore a two-piece romper suit. Johann helped his daughter hold the baby and told everyone how proud he was to have his children there.

Reports of fighting in Russia dominated the radio news. Johann knew it was now no longer a matter of *if* he was going to have to serve on active duty, but of *when*. There was supposed to be a big push into Russia, and reports stated that the German army was convinced that in a short time, Russia would be defeated. In the village, the Nazis increased their pressure on the local men to serve. They reminded Johann often to think about his family, especially his daughter. She would be starting school soon, and they pointed out that she might miss this opportunity if he did not make his contribution.

His son grew quickly, and each day his mother-in-law recounted to him what baby Johann did during the day. His daughter was learning to write, and each evening he spent time with her on his lap holding her hand as she pushed the pencil on the slate to make each letter. His wife remembers how much he would praise her after each one. He smiled when her letter began to take shape, and she would tell him what she wrote or drew. He could always tell what the letters were before she told him, but that did not prevent him from acting surprised, as if he could not guess. He felt blessed by this wonderful life in Heidendorf, and he often told his wife that he could not wait until the fall when his daughter would begin school.

Thoughts of war seemed far removed from his life as Johann focused on his family. He drew up plans and then built a table and chair for his growing daughter. His wife remembers that he had intended to paint them a nice yellow and then repaint little Anna's highchair so that his son would have something that appeared new, even if it was not. The summer passed quickly, and he had many small tasks and chores that he wanted to finish, many of them were overdue. Johann replaced and then expanded the chicken coop. He built new shelves for his wife and stepmother to store the preserves and other food. He also expanded the horse's stall so that it had more space to move around. He told Anna that time was of the essence because each year the children were getting bigger and they needed to work harder to accommodate their growing family. He never mentioned it, but Anna is certain that at the time he was thinking he would have to leave soon.

In 1942, Johann was adamant that he would not join the army – at least not the German army, and so as a means of persuading him to change his mind, the head of the Nazis in Heidendorf declared that little Anna could not begin classes that year. Since she was only four years old, Johann told them that it did not matter; she did not need to go yet. Johann heard from some of the men in the village who travelled to other places that denying access to schooling was a favourite tactic of the Nazis, to force the men to fight. He was livid and told his wife that they would teach their daughter at home. Since the local teacher was a close companion of Johann's, they made an agreement that his little Anna could receive her schoolwork in the evenings. Different members of their families would visit Johann's house each night and deliver her lessons. They hoped the Nazi men would not suspect anything, and Johann could continue to refuse to go to an unjust war.

Baby Johann was growing and soon he would turn one. He learned to walk by supporting himself on the furniture around the house, causing chaos in the process by pulling down the tablecloths. Johann was quick to come to his son's defence, saying that little Anna had done the same thing as well. The baby would also grab on to his father's trousers as a means to walk and stand up while Johann walked through the house. He kept telling Anna that little Johann's dress needed to be replaced with short pants. Anna pointed out that he was not quite one yet, and she did not want to lose her baby to boyhood before she had to. She remembers how much Johann loved his two children, and it saddened him to think that his children might face the wrath of strangers for his choice of not serving in the army.

Johann kept a brave face, but his wife and her siblings remember that he seemed to know that if circumstances changed, if he needed to go and fight, there would be a reckoning between him and the Nazis in the village. He once told his wife how much he despised them – they valued everything that he loathed. They believed in the power of the Führer and of the righteous power of Germany, and in hatred of Jews and other people of non-German origins. The Nazis did not agree with religion, and with their songs and chants, they seemed bent on removing the church from people's lives. Anna recalls no other time when he was quite so angry and so passionate. Still there was good news: another addition to the family, due in the summer of 1944, distracted Johann from worrying. Anna remembers how excited he was, perhaps more so than she, but he told her not to mention it to anyone outside of their own families.

She kept quiet, but someone who knew must have accidentally said something in the presence of people who should not know. The Nazi men pressed their advantage.

Anna is certain that one of the Nazis came up to one of the houses and overheard a conversation about the upcoming arrival. There was no other way they could have learned of her pregnancy. They sent for Johann and informed him that he needed to join the army, and it had to be soon. When once again he refused, they told him that they would send his wife and children to labour camps. Anna remembers that they did not quite put it this way, but by this time everyone knew that so-called "undesirable" people were disappearing and that men who balked at joining the German Army found themselves faced with a similar ultimatum. He told Anna that he would never allow this to happen to his family, and he would therefore join the army. Anna remembers how they both cried well into the night. She believed that he would die. He assured her that he would survive military service. She did not believe him, especially after the leader of the Nazi men came to inform Johann that he was to leave in December that year. Johann never told her precisely what they said, but she could make a good guess from the delight on the man's face as he gave this ultimatum to her beloved. Even though the village pastor spoke of God's peace each Sunday in church, Anna remembers that she felt that there was no sense of peace in her home. The message in his sermons was to find peace and forgive, but she could not. Her husband was leaving for Russia, a country that seemed dauntingly all-powerful.

Her daughter did not understand when they told her that her father would be leaving for a while, and that she would be able to go to school. Little Anna was not one to ask too many questions; she was like her father in that she thought long and hard before speaking. When she finally formed a question, she asked why her father had to leave. She clung to Johann. His son did the same. Although he was certainly too young to form a strong memory of his father or an understanding of what was going on around him, he nonetheless seemed to see that everyone was unhappy. His Uncle Peter had already left, and was near

Russia, and Anna recalls that each time Johann left the room, his son would shout, "no!" She thinks that this was his way of telling his father not to go.

Johann departed after Christmas. Anna remembers that he left at night so as not to upset the children. He feared that he would not be able to go if the children started to cry. Even so, he cried as he went into their room and gently tucked them in. He kissed his son, gazing at his cherub-like face, smiling. He looked at his son touched his cheek, and kissed his head. He sat down by his daughter's bed. He re-fixed her covers. He touched her cheek as well. He did not move or speak, but Anna is certain that he was telling his daughter how much he loved her. Anna saw that he was praying. Finally, he leaned over and whispered in his daughter's ear, kissed her cheek and fixed the covers again. Before he left the room, he looked at them both as if to memorize their faces.

Anna remembers that she did not cry because she wanted to show her husband how brave she was. They embraced, and he told her to take care of his children and herself. He told her he loved her and the children, and he wanted nothing to happen to her. He gazed into her eyes, as if attempting to memorize her face too, and he gently kissed her lips. He whispered in her ear that he loved her always, and she should be brave. He opened the door as quietly as he could, gave her his gentle smile, and left, shutting the door as softly as he could so as not to wake the children. She remembers that it was only after she was certain that he had left that she fell on her knees and wept.

Anna received several letters from Johann. He was in training; he did not say where. He even sent her a newspaper clipping of a photo he was in. He wrote that he loved her and he told her to take care of his children. She wrote back in the same vein. She prayed and hoped for the best. Perhaps the war would end, and her beloved would return. They would farm and have more children.

Then a letter came from Johann telling her that his company was heading east, to Russia. Anna noted that he never mentioned how he was treated in the army. She was not sure what to make of it; perhaps the letter was censored before it was delivered to her.

Anna did not hear much news of what came later. What she did learn came through her brother, Peter, and a friend of Johann's who was in the same company, Thomas. The company boarded a train to Russia. It made stops along the way to pick up more men and supplies. The men were crowded into small, dark rail cars that sped towards Russia, and some felt certain of their fate. Once they got past the German-controlled borders, they knew that they might die. Thomas recalls that many men were fearful of this prospect. Johann dreaded being far away, and he feared losing the freedom to be with his wife and children more than he feared death. On the train, the soldiers did not talk much. Their minds focused on other things: their families, friends and homes. After several days of darkness inside the train, they stopped in Riga, a city in Russian controlled territory. The train doors opened and, from what the friend reported, Johann was one of the first men to disembark. The cold air coupled with the sudden bright sunlight and dazzling snow proved fatal.

Thomas can only guess that Johann must have blinked or moved too slowly, or that something shone from his pack. There was a sniper in the nearby brush. The man took aim and discharged his weapon. Johann was shot and killed by this sniper. Johann did not fire a single shot. He kept his promise not to kill, and the price of this promise was his death. Thomas does not remember what part of Johann's body sustained the fatal injury, but it did not matter, for Johann was dead before he hit the ground.

The same sniper shot at Thomas as well, and he lost his leg. The commanders of Johann's unit were quick to find the sniper's hiding place. They exacted retribution in the form of an immediate execution, but more men were already dead or severely wounded. Anna reflects bitterly that the sniper was good at his work. Anna is certain that even in death Johann would not have wanted more suffering, either of the other men in his company or of the sniper.

Word of Johann's death did not come back to her from any official source but from Thomas who, once he was able, passed it through other channels.

Anna remembers growing more anxious by the day. There were no letters or telegrams coming to the family. She wondered what might have happened to Johann to make him stop writing to them. She feared it was because he was dead, but she did not want to accept that idea. She wanted his strong arms around her, and to hear him tell her that everything was all right. She needed him here for his children, and for her. One evening her aunt and her brother Michael came to visit. She normally enjoyed Michael's visits since he was so light-hearted and joyful. He always brought a smile to her face. That evening, though, Michael seemed distant and preoccupied. He did not say much to her, and he kept walking in and out of the house. He seemed concerned with some piece of news, and he took his aunt outside where they spoke for a while.

Anna remembers how she felt; as if there was the gentle presence of her husband, telling her things would be all right. It was as if he was giving her permission to continue with her life. She thought of him and his smile, his laughter, his demeanour. When her aunt returned, she broke the news of Johann's death to her. She was quick to add that he had not suffered, and that Anna needed to be strong. For her children's sake, she must become both mother and father to them until the right time. Anna understood this meant that when she was ready, she should remarry. She decided, though, that her beloved had been taken from her, and she would never remarry. She convinced herself that, at twenty-five, she was too old to remarry.

She remembers how bitter she was when the army did not return any of Johann's personal belongings. She wanted to send letters to someone demanding that they return something, anything: a reminder, a memento, his wedding ring. Most of all, she wanted his wedding ring, the one she had so joyfully placed upon his finger seven years before. Her father told her that the same thing happened when his brother died, and it would be best to save what little she could for her children. She took his advice and placed everything that had meant something to Johann in a chest for her children. It was all for the children. They needed it, especially the baby, who would never meet his father and the other two who had lost their father before they should have.

Betrayed by the Nazis, she refused to acknowledge their condolences, preferring to believe that they had caused her suffering. She saw that her family followed suit, and whenever they could, they deliberately failed to acknowledge the presence of these men. Her father was bolder, and called the men "cowards." More than a few members of the family expressed relief when the Nazis left the village. She did not know how to tell her children that their father would never come home. She remembers that she did manage to tell them somehow, but cannot recall that now. Little Anna took to sitting by the mulberry bush waiting and looking down the road after school; she too could not believe that her father was gone forever. Little Johann cried and looked for his father's strong arms. He seemed to want to be tucked in each night, but not in the way Anna did it. Anna realized that little Johann wanted to be tucked in the way his father did before he left on that final night. Her son relaxed once she attempted to do it that way, perhaps sensing her intentions.

Her second son was born four months later, and Anna wanted to baptize him with a name that Johann would have liked. She broke with tradition by giving her son two names, "Michael" after her brother and her deceased uncle, and "Thomas" after Johann's close friend. In honouring both men, she prayed that Johann would be pleased with the choices. She remembers that he had always loved his young brother-in-law, Michael, who would also be lost to her. He left before his namesake nephew was born, and he would die in Budapest. Anna could not remember another year that was so eventful.

That September in 1944, with her three children, she was forced to flee from her home.[14] She packed the letters and photos for her children and the last Romanian money that Johann had sent her into a chest along with some winter clothes. The army's assurances that she would be able to return to the village later meant nothing to her, for now she doubted anything they said. They had been a part of the Nazis' plan to send her husband to a certain death, and she therefore distrusted their promises. Anna, her children and her sister boarded a train, and they migrated back to the land of their ancestors, Germany.

She tried to make a new life for herself there. She learned from her brother Peter that her sister-in-law, Johann's younger sister, was still alive and had returned to Romania following incarceration in a Russian labour camp. Her sister-in-law's decision that "she would not bother Anna or the children" grieved her. Anna still believes that her sister-in-law perhaps felt hurt and feared being rejected. Anna muses that the labour camp may have destroyed her sister-in-law's spirit. She worries that her sister-in-law simply gave up hope of finding her own happiness. Whatever the reason, it created an infinite sadness in Anna. Another tie with her husband was gone, lost to her forever.

Later the family moved to Canada because her father decided that they would not be divided again when her younger sister, Maria, became engaged and was planning to move there. Once in Canada, Anna attempted to bury her feelings and memories of Johann by focussing on caring for her children and her work. She avoided speaking about Johann because the memories were too painful. Any attempt at thinking about him resulted in a flood of tears. Finally, the pain was unbearable and she felt that it was best just to forget. She asked her daughter Anna about her memories of Heidendorf, and of her father. Little Anna told her that she could not remember much, just the mulberry bushes; she had no memories of her father. Anna decided that since her oldest child could not remember her father then Anna would not speak of him. It was as if her children did not want to talk about him, and if that was the case, she decided not to push the issue. If he were not important to them, she would not force his memory on them. Yet, she could not forget him: his smile, his touch, his voice, his love for her. Too many wonderful memories of a life cut short.

Now she is uncertain whether her children said that they could not remember him for fear of hurting her, or simply because they genuinely could not recall him. She tried to remarry when her youngest son Michael was ten, but her daughter was not sure if she should, and so she did not remarry. Later she tucked Johann's letters, and that newspaper clipping with his photo in a safe place, and it was not until one of her granddaughters asked about them that she showed them to another living soul. The rest of the family showed no interest – much to her dismay. She realized that they could not know how much she loved him. Later when she moved out of her home, the letters went missing. She believes that during the move someone threw the small cardboard box with the letters and Romanian money in it in the garbage. The only things she has now are the pictures of Johann. It was too late.

Yet, she muses, perhaps not. It gives her peace, she says, that at least one person wanted to know about Johann. It also helps that the name is still carried within the family, through her son and his grandchildren. It helps that she can tell people to see what her children have become: strong, beautiful, and intelligent. She kept her promise to him to care for them. It saddens her that their father never got the chance to see this and that she never gave her children the opportunity, at least until now, to know about their father. She fears that they will be far from interested, or worse, not care. Still, it only takes one. In a sense, he left her early for a reason: later in her life she lost a tiny infant great-grandchild, so he is in Heaven with his great-grandfather, except, she comments ruefully, they were each taken from her about eighty years too soon.

She leans back in her chair and smiles. I look at her and then I wrap my hand around hers. She looks at me and says, you know, he had brown eyes. None of my children had brown eyes, but most of my grandchildren do, and so do my great-grandchildren. One looks so much like him, the same smile, and the same eyes. She stops for a moment, pondering her final question to me. Do I think that she loved Johann? I nod, knowing her answer already.

A Home of One's Own

The angry roar of the water rings in his ears, and the worst of his fears comes true as Peter and his companion approach the river. The bridge was bombed and nothing but rubble remains in the angry foaming water. Peter glances around to see if there was any other way to get across the river – perhaps there is a boat, or a long branch he could use to pull himself across it. There is nothing, and the only way home is to swim. He tells his friend that there is a problem: He does not know how to swim.

The river is deep and wide and, the water races over huge chunks of concrete and twisted metal; it is not a good time to learn to swim. His friend looks at him and begins to take off his shoes and socks and tie them in a bag. Then he asks if Peter wants to go home after everything he has already been through? Wordlessly Peter begins to remove his boots. He is not afraid to die – not anymore, but a bullet to the head would be a faster and less painful death.

Peter proclaims with a wave of his hand that time is running out. He is nearly ninety now; older than he ever thought he might become. Although his body is older, his mind still is sharp, so I should not try to question his accuracy too much. People still trust his memories of events and dates. He is old enough to have survived events that many can never understand. He has lived in more countries than he thought was ever possible, and after the death of his beloved wife, he simply wants to tell his story and her story – really their story, their true story. He will tell me that there are two others who were lost to him so long ago, and he needs to tell me about them as well. He wants them back in his life once more, and to him they are almost alive. His eyes tear up as he glances my way.

He has a lot to tell me about his life, and to do so he sits in his comfortable old couch. He directs my gaze at another couch. Sit there, he commands, pointing to it. I sit. He explains to me why he sits where he sits. From there he can look out at his garden and make certain that the squirrels do not make much of a mess, but after he cut down the grape vines a few years ago, there is less chance of that happening.

He smiles as he remembers the hours of work it took to clean the fallen grapes and vines, and the squirrels jumping at him to annoy him. He had important plans that day: a picnic with his wife Sofia. He was furious about the mess. Beside him is a picture of him and his wife that was taken some twenty years earlier, and he figures that he has not changed all that much. His hair is thinner and greyer, but it is not white. His glasses and frames are newer, but his smile is the same. His brown eyes twinkle in the same mischievous way, although there are more wrinkles around them. His belly is bigger, but in some ways that is to be expected for someone who is close to ninety and cannot exercise even though the doctor has told him to do it for his health. Grinning, he asks me, whom is he trying to impress? I laugh and tell him, certainly not me.

I ask about his life, and shrugging his shoulders and pushing up his glasses he asks me, what do I want to know? Everything, I reply. He tells me to get comfortable, he will take his time, and he will tell me everything. He punctuates his story with sips of water and by getting up to show me a picture or two. He will proclaim to anyone who will listen that his life is rather boring, but if they want to know, he will bore them. He grins when he says this, as if he has a secret that he wants to share with his listeners.

Peter, true to his word, begins at the beginning.

As the snow began to melt on the hills cradling the small village of Heidendorf,[15] in March 1921, a young woman gave birth to her second child and first son. She had celebrated her twentieth birthday less than three months earlier, but the impending birth overshadowed any festivities for her birthday. There was no specific concern about the upcoming arrival that dampened them; just the fact that she was going to have a baby soon, and she did not need to overexert herself at this time. The young mother was healthy before the birth, labour progressed quickly, and she and her newborn son recovered in the comfort of their family home where he was born.

In Heidendorf, the midwife came to all the births because the village did not have a doctor[16]. It was also expensive to call a doctor for something people considered a dangerous but natural event. Although there had been no recent deaths of babies or mothers, it had happened before. The midwife told his mother that since the labour was quick and the baby was strong this was a good omen. God would protect him and give him strength for the future.

His parents decided on a small but important matter long before he was born. His father's name was Peter and, as the eldest son, this boy's name would be Peter, too. This followed a tradition that dated back long before even his father's birth in 1889. Peter was a common first name in many Heidendorf families, and this often caused confusion for outsiders and merriment for the people who tried to tell stories involving several different people with the same name. With several generations alive simultaneously in a family, a name could be used by more than one relative or neighbour. To get around the difficulties of having the same names, many family members would adopt a village nickname. For now, swaddled and sleeping in a wooden cradle, baby Peter was simply called Peter by family members and villagers alike. In time, he would develop a nickname that he would use for most of his adult life, Younger Peter. The path his life he would take was already decided by his cultural history and the community. He would be a farmer.

Peter made his first public appearance in the village church. At four weeks old, he received the sacrament of Holy Baptism.

As Peter grew, the events of the church and any other special occasions always meant a different meal from what he normally ate. They would gather around the dinner table with extended family and friends, and there would be singing and laughter the whole night. Even as young as two, Peter loved singing along with his father to the songs that he knew. His family would teach him many things as he grew into manhood.

His immediate family continued to grow. He had an older sister named Anna, and in late 1922, his mother gave birth to his younger sister Sofia. Peter recalls that Sofia was quiet and she never squirmed in his arms when his mother held both of them on her lap. In 1924, she gave birth to his brother, Michael. Then in 1927, she gave birth to his sister Maria. Once Michael turned one and was old enough to wear short pants, their mother dressed him in Peter's hand-me-downs. Peter was happy that as the older brother he received all of the new clothes. The one thing he disliked was that he had to take his brother along with him everywhere. His grandmother or mother would often ask him to do it, but Peter always hoped that Michael would stay with his elder sister. Michael never did, though, or wanted to for that matter. Peter did not like the work involved in taking his brother everywhere. Michael was always wandering off or asking too many questions. Shortly after Maria's birth, Peter complained to his mother that Maria was loud. His mother replied that Maria only cried when she was hungry or needed her diaper changed. He accepted this reason without argument, and he was pleased when his mother told him that Michael was louder.

The arrival of his sister was not the only new thing to happen to him that year. In the autumn of the year he turned five, about four months before Maria's birth, he began attending the Heidendorf School. He felt more grown up now since he could go to classes while his younger brother Michael had to stay with their grandmother. He could tell Michael wanted to join him, and he seemed to try to negotiate with their grandmother to allow him to go to school, too. Peter overheard them talking about the grand adventure that school was, and how much Michael wanted to join Peter there. He recalls thinking that his brother likely just wanted to bother him with his presence in class. Spending time at school during the day proved more enjoyable than he had imagined since his friends also attended.

Because learning was very highly valued by his parents and his village, Peter spent most of his day inside the classroom. His older sister Anna started school two years before Peter. Since he was a boy, the teacher did not intentionally compare him to his sister, but she was not as active in the games the children played outside, and the teacher would comment regularly on how nice and quiet his sister was by comparison.

He liked his teacher, and he appreciated the strong friendships he made during the year. Before the year began, he imagined that he would learn German language and history all day, that it would be fun learning about rulers of the past, and that the class would only study these two subjects. He was mistaken.

Peter learned math and another language, Romanian,[17] but he felt that they would not be of any benefit to him in his adult life, and he only wanted to learn German. Romanian was difficult for him to pronounce and foreign sounding to his ears, and it had too many rules to be enjoyable. It was not as melodic-sounding as the German or the Saxon dialect that he spoke at home. After much thought, and a conversation with his teacher, he decided that since he lived in Romania, he would need to use the language when he grew up or if he continued his education outside of the village, and so he learned it. He also discovered that mathematics was helpful for some things like counting wheat bags and deciding how many logs to bring in each day. He valued the ability to read and to write in the German language.

Although history lessons required him to memorize dates and names, he found them intriguing, especially when they pertained to Transylvania or the Saxon people. He knew that his homeland was once a part of Hungary, but it became a part of

Romania in 1919 at the conclusion of the First World War. After that war, the Romanians allowed the Saxon people to keep their German culture and language, but they must now teach Romanian to their children as well.[18] In order to continue teaching, all of the Saxon teachers were required to learn Romanian and teach it to their students in the villages. For centuries, his teacher explained, people could learn Hungarian, Romanian and formal German in the major cities. The other point the teacher made was that tradition stated only men would do professional work like teaching in a village school or university or becoming a church minister.

Peter later learned that the national government was making a push towards the "Romanianization" of the population of Transylvania[19], which consisted of Romanians, Hungarians, Germans, and many other ethnic groups.

Young Peter had an optimistic outlook concerning changes within his community and the wider world. He believed that there would always be new siblings, cousins, and friends to play with and that he would grow healthy and strong. He refused to believe that growing up also had its trials.

In the waning summer days of 1927, Peter, his sisters Anna and Sofia, and his brother Michael fell ill with what appeared to be simple colds. When the high fevers began, it became apparent that it was much more serious. Peter found that he had a great deal of trouble swallowing even the softest food, and he often wanted to sleep. He had a headache and coughing fits. The coughing bothered him the most. His ribs hurt and he had more trouble breathing. He overheard his parents talking quietly and he learned that his brother and sisters were suffering in the same way. Peter saw the look of concern on his parents' faces, and he heard the whispered conversations each night. He grew frustrated that his mother and aunts would not allow him to do his chores or to go outside. He wanted to do something, but since he felt so weak, he could not. He did not want his parents to worry – after all, he was almost six, and he was a young, strong boy and the eldest son. He tried to stay out of bed for as long as he could, but his mother kept insisting that he rest, much to his chagrin.

His parents worried and prayed. They dared not come close to the children and Peter could not understand why. His parents knew the sickness was diphtheria,[20] a highly contagious disease. It could suffocate children and adults, and it could be fatal if they became too weak to cough up the membrane blocking their airways. Peter heard his parents talk to his aunts who came to the house frequently. Then his mother took him aside and explained to him that she, his youngest sister, and his father must leave the house for a while, until all of the children were healthy again.

By leaving for a short time, his parents and baby sister Maria might remain healthy and safe since they had never had diphtheria; the aunts who stayed had fought this sickness before, so they would not get sick again. Peter would later learn that this was a common myth in the village, and his aunts were actually risking their own lives to look after their nieces and nephews. He watched his aunts' daily chores closely. They kept the fires going all the time and heated water to keep the air in the house humid. Peter was still burning from the fever, and he resented the further heat that the fire produced.

Peter's recovery from diphtheria was faster than his aunts had anticipated. Although he was still weak, he wanted to get out of bed, and he tried to sneak out. Many times his aunt Maria would find him and bring him back. She told him that the cold coming in from the windows and door was not good for him and she promised to give him her best homemade candy if he stayed in bed. Peter accepted this arrangement because he loved the candy his aunt made. His older sister Anna recovered quickly as well. Soon only his brother Michael and sister Sofia were ill. Peter felt stronger each day.

With this strength came the ability to take in his unbearably hot, damp surroundings. He could not understand why his aunts still kept it hot, but then he noticed that his younger siblings did not recover as quickly as he did. His aunts allowed him to look through the window each day, but they forbade him to leave the house. When he saw that the corn was almost ready to harvest, he encouraged his two younger siblings to get well so that they might help their parents. He told his younger sister that school would start soon and that she needed to be well to join him. He recalls she did not even have enough energy to move, to nod, or to look at him because she was so weak from the sickness.

With his older sister and his aunts, he prayed to God for the recovery of his brother and sister. Each night he prayed, and as soon as he awoke, he prayed. After many days, his brother slowly regained his health and he believed that his prayers were being answered. Only Sofia remained ill. Her coughing lessened as she grew weaker, and her breathing was raspy and laboured.

Since all the children were still contagious, Peter overheard his aunt's frantic assertions that the risk to take the children to a doctor in Bistritz was too high: they could not go, and the journey might kill them. As Sofia's condition deteriorated, Peter told his aunts that they needed to go to Bistritz whatever the risk. His aunts gently told him that this was the best decision they could make; they did not want to hurt any of the children. To help Sofia, his aunts would raise her little body higher by placing more down filled pillows beneath her head and shoulders. They also kept the water boiling all the time in order to increase the humidity and heat inside the house. Peter longed to help, and his aunts told him that the best thing he could do was to stay healthy and pray for his sister. He prayed each morning when he woke up and again at night before he fell into a dreamless sleep.

Sofia did not get better, and as much as he prayed, his little sister still died. Her fever was too high and she could no longer cough. Peter felt devastated, and he decided that God was to blame. Michael got well with his prayers, and he asked one of his aunts why his sister did not. In a vain effort to comfort him, she told him that it was God's will, and that his sister was with the angels in heaven because God needed her there. He missed her, and he missed his parents who could not come home and comfort their own children for fear of contracting the illness.

Sofia's funeral took place within a few days in the village church, but Peter, Anna and Michael could not attend. They were still contagious and physically weak. As the tiny coffin adorned with white and yellow marigolds passed the house, Peter peeked through the window and through his tears as his sister made her final journey to the Saxon cemetery just outside of the village. When he regained his health, one of the first things that Peter and his surviving siblings did was to go to the cemetery and place flowers on his sister's grave.

They always brought marigolds to her grave because they were his sister's favourite flower. Peter found a way to remember his sister by always having marigolds near him whenever he could.

Once Peter regained his health and was able to do most of his chores again, life returned to its former rhythm, but the memories of recent events left him with a changed perception of the world. Even though life would continue for him, he no longer assumed that it would unfold according to a well laid out plan. He understood that it was not good to question his parents about Sofia's death because it would cause his mother to cry. Peter did not like to see his mother upset so he usually avoided speaking about her. As they offered their condolences, many of the villagers told his parents that this was God's will, and by way of a reply, his parents would smile wanly. Peter despised the phrase, but it seemed to him that it comforted the family and in particular his mother. As time passed, she often told her remaining healthy children that they were a blessing to her. Peter thought of Sofia with a hint of sadness because she would have started school this year, and his sadness grew when he saw his mother put away Sofia's schoolbooks and a chalkboard into a trunk one evening.

After Sofia's death in 1927, the family grew again with the birth of two more sisters, Katharina in 1928 and Sofia in 1930.

By the time Sofia was born in 1930, his life as a farmer was well on course. His final three years at the school were upon him, and then he would begin the life that he was born to lead – in training, his father often reminded him.

Because Peter was the oldest son, but not yet an adult in the eyes of the village, his father allowed him to listen to conversations the men had about life in the village and the outside world, but Peter was not to speak about the events that were happening in Germany and Austria. These events seemed to be of great significance to the older men of Heidendorf who debated the subject over wine and food.

In 1934, by the time Peter completed his final school year, the Austrian-born Adolf Hitler came to power in Germany. Hitler talked about the greatness of Germany and the German people, the fact that they had been humiliated by other countries, and that they needed to regain their power once again. He promised to make this happen, and he felt that many countries needed to learn that Germany had a strong military force.

Peter could tell that many of the village men, including his teacher, felt that Saxons in Transylvania deserved some respite from the high taxes and loss of land. After the collapse of the Austrian Empire, the treaty of Trianon in 1920 ceded Transylvania to Romania. Although the Saxon people paid high taxes before the treaty was signed, they now paid significantly more to the victorious side, the Romanian people, and this placed a great burden on the Saxon farmers. Hitler promised what Peter and the Saxon people needed: hope and pride. Peter recalls that some argued that nothing would change, but others said it certainly would because Hitler talked about the German peoples, and the Saxons were Germanic in origin[21].

Not all of these comments and discussions that the men had and had again were as exciting as Peter hoped, and he had a more pressing matter to attend to: his impending confirmation. This confirmation into the Lutheran Church took place on Palm Sunday – the week before Easter. On that day, each boy and girl who turned thirteen or fourteen that year faced an examination of their knowledge of doctrine and faith in the Lutheran Church. After they passed this examination, they received a blessing and had communion from the pastor and became adults in the eyes of the villagers of Heidendorf. There was never a child who failed, though all of them were nervous. Peter had a special outfit, called a Tracht Hemd, made for this occasion, and he would now wear it every Sunday to church and when he went dancing in the village hall. It was a long-sleeved white shirt with intricate black stitching around the collar and at the wrists. He wore it with a black tie that had more intricate stitching in brighter colours. After the confirmation service ended, the family went back to their house for a dinner and other entertainment.

His father loved to sing, and he entertained their guests with his wonderful voice. This day was the highlight of his youth. Since his family was poor, he received no expensive gifts, and there were no photographs taken in honour of this milestone event. Peter did not receive anything beyond immense pride in his accomplishment. The next time he expected to have this much attention showered on him would be at his wedding. He began to feel that since he was older now, people looked upon him with different expectations. He dismissed his childhood worries because he was now a young adult, and he had best act like one. To his unending irritation, reality began to intrude on his well-laid plans.

His small world soon faced another challenge, and the decisions and actions of other people altered the life he was intending to lead. The changes around him forced him to rethink his expectations of the future.

In 1938, Austria and Germany were unified into one large country by public voting in Austria[22] and it was now called Greater Germany. The same year he heard, on the radio in Heidendorf, about the Munich agreement that gave a part of Czechoslovakia to Germany. He heard about the Prime Minister of Britain, Neville Chamberlain, who announced that peace was given to the world with this agreement. This angered Peter since up until that point it seemed that Britain wanted nothing more than to fight. He recalls that some men disagreed with the declaration, and they thought that Germany was strong enough to force Britain into submission should there be a war.

The radio announcements told of how Germany and Hungary were gaining back land that was rightfully theirs. Over the course of that year, he learned that Hungary received a portion of its territory from Czechoslovakia without a war, and this hand-over would become known as the Vienna Awards. His fears began to take hold as he realized that what was once a simple required three-year exercise of being a soldier was quickly becoming more dangerous. The danger of his death from a bullet, however, would not happen for a number of years at the age of twenty-one. Since he was not yet close to that age, he could concentrate on something more productive: the goings on of the village.

He enjoyed the dances that the village held regularly. The girls always seemed to want to dance with him, but he knew that everyone danced with whoever was not dancing. Since he did not attend school any more like his younger siblings, he could go to dances early and stay out as late as he pleased. Although he was willing to have more education, the family did not have the money to do so. Peter believed he was a good dancer, but when he stepped on his dancing partner's toes, he would apologize and say that his boots were too big. Many of the women enjoyed his fine voice, and with this encouragement, he would often sing to them.

Peter watched Michael as he grew and was keen to see his personality develop. Peter was disappointed to discover that it was distinctly different from his own. Peter remembers being more like his mother – reserved and quiet. Michael was more outgoing and viewed life differently; his personality was closer to that of their father. These days, he felt that his father was too joyful and not as serious as he should be, given the current world events, and lately Michael seemed to be thinking the same way. He decided that since Michael would soon be old enough to join the young people's group in the village it was best not to dwell on their differences too much.

He distracted himself by being involved in the dances and the singing in the evening. For now, he felt secure in getting to know the girls of the village and listening to the radio. He hunted for information about the world situation. To his dismay, the world intruded again.

The political boundaries changed, and this time it affected him far more than he could imagine. There would not be a war; rather, it would be a negotiated transfer of lands between Hungary and Romania, and many people felt grateful for this.

Hungary wanted its lost territory back and the men within it[23]. He knew that his tall, strong farmer's build was not suited to being a specialized soldier, a sniper or a tank gunner. He was not going to be an officer, he was not of the proper social standing, and this meant that the army would place him in the front lines.

The largest area that Hungary lost was Transylvania, in 1920, and now they wanted it back. There was a great debate among the men about what might happen to the village if a border war broke out between Romania and Hungary. Peter secretly hoped for a lasting peace – not so much for the world but for himself. He would not turn twenty-one yet in 1942, but he worried that he might be required to serve in the army sooner since he was born in March. When he found spare time, he enjoyed the company of people his age or he listened to the radio with the rest of the men in Heidendorf.

He recalls that King Carol of Romania[24] would often broadcast announcements over the radio, and he usually talked about himself. Peter recalls how much this bored him, because the King never seemed to care about anything except his own greatness. Then, the announcer moved on to the state of world affairs. He reported on European affairs, mostly, and he did not often mention Asia or America. This was how Peter heard about what was happening in Poland and Germany[25].

Peter recalls that he did not hear many official reports about German policy, their true military might, how the Nazis intended to fight a war, or what Hitler needed to do to regain all the land he promised to the German people. What he heard, frequently, was that the Treaty of Versailles was designed to humiliate the proud German people. Romania supported Germany but did not want to go to war.

Peter believed that a war would destroy everything he worked for – his land and his life. He knew how much land the Saxons once owned. It had changed hands many times, and it was not producing as well under the care of the farmers who now owned it. He did not want to hear about fighting on the radio, either in Romania or anywhere else, since it would mean that he might be called into service sooner than he expected. He found that hope dashed, and war soon broke out.

In September of 1939, the war between Germany and Poland began. Peter feared the prospect of continued fighting. Romania was quick to declare neutrality, and Peter was grateful. From the stories his father told, if war escalated, it would not matter to the army if he were twenty-one yet or not. The radio announced that even though Britain and France had declared war on Germany over its invasion of Poland, there were no major battles between Germany and France. Men in the village said that Russia was not declaring war against Germany. Peter said many prayers of thanks that there was no major fighting between these mighty countries. Peter suspected that, if France and Germany were to fight for a long time, his mandatory service to the Romanian army would send him to France, where he would be injured or killed in the trenches.

Then, incredibly, France was defeated. The radio announcers told the men of Heidendorf that France had surrendered to Germany and peace would soon come. The mighty and powerful French army was beaten and humiliated. The war was over before it began, and Germany was victorious. It did not occur to Peter that Britain was still in the war, but he recalls that it was France and its large army that worried most people in Heidendorf. Peter was so happy he hugged everyone he saw, including his brother. Life was normal again and he would join the Romanian army in a world at peace. He would finish his service with a bit of money and this would help when, in time, he started a family. He hoped that this victory would allow for more freedoms for the Saxons in Romania. With a stronger Germany, perhaps his dreams would come true. He began to hear more rumours about changes, but to his delight, they were good.

In 1940, Hungary and Romania made a territorial change – without a war. The news reporter on the radio told the villagers that Romania would give the northern part of Transylvania to Hungary while the southern part would remain a part of Romania. Peter was now Hungarian, and he thought hard about what this really meant to him.

As the men of Heidendorf debated the merits of Hungarian rule, he found that his opinion about joining the army changed. Where before, he knew he would go into the Romanian army at the age of twenty-one (the next year), he was now not sure what the Hungarian army would ask of him. He hoped that it would be the same, but he also knew that Hungary was an ally of Germany and could soon be drawn into the war. He recalls that because he was young and healthy, he knew that he would be called to serve as a soldier no matter what he wanted. After years of work on the farm and carrying heavy equipment from the house up the hills to the fields, he was strong. He remembered hearing from his brother-in-law, Johann, that obeying orders was important as well.

And then he had something more important to worry about – his father's health.

His father took ill with what seemed to be the flu or a bad cold. Later he learnt it was pneumonia and then typhoid fever.

His father needed to rest in bed for weeks. Peter recalls how bitter he felt that his mother needed to care for his father in addition to her many other daily responsibilities. He kept hearing his father coughing at night, and he saw his mother placing cold compresses on his head. To his horror, he dreamt that his father died. He recalled that the last time he had prayed for a person's survival was for his sister Sofia and she died. He was unsure his father would survive, and he kept hoping that he would. For weeks, his father lay ill in bed. Planting the wheat and corn became Peter's responsibility until his father recovered.

He waited for his father's health to improve. Finally, it did, and for this, Peter was grateful, but he did not pray too much in thanks. He seemed to think this was a way to make God angry with him, and the result of this anger would be his father's death. He felt that when the harvest time came, his father would help him as much as he could. He kept this in the back of his mind, and when he thought about it, he smiled. He was proud to have so much responsibility for this year's harvest because it proved he was a man and could handle the heavy workload of a farmer. But, once again, his father fell ill.

At first, Peter thought it was nothing, but he saw that his father could not carry anything for a long distance without dropping it and stopping to breathe. He would sweat and, waving his hand in dismissal, tell them he was all right. Sofia, Maria, and Katharina tried to take over as much of the workload as they could between them, but Peter often needed to help when the girls could not. His father did not get up one day to help with the harvest and his mother worried for his life. At first, they gave his father the home remedies to help with colds – broth and strong tea – but nothing helped. Peter feared that his father was ill with the dreaded diphtheria that claimed his sister, the elder Sofia, so many years before. However, his father once again had typhoid, and Peter was uncertain if it was a new attack or if his father never recovered from the original attack in the spring.

Then there was something more. Peter refused to admit that he was ill, but in the last few weeks, he found it more and more difficult to harvest the corn or the wheat. The weakness in his body continued to grow worse.

He is unsure of the exact day that it happened, but it was near the end of the harvest; Peter felt much worse and told his brother-in-law Johann that he could not finish because he was feeling so weak. He headed straight home. To his dismay, he too had typhoid. The next week Peter could not remember much, and he only recalls that it took him another three weeks before he could muster enough strength to get out of bed. His father also recovered his strength, but being over fifty, his recovery was slower in comparison to Peter.

The first thing that Peter did when he recovered was thank his brother Michael and brother-in-law Johann for their work in the fields during his illness. They both told him not to think of it, and he believes that his uncles gained a new appreciation for Michael. Peter had always thought that Michael was irresponsible, and they were all pleased with Michael's work ethic this year.

The weather changed during the course of Peter's illness. Far earlier than expected, it snowed in Heidendorf.

The constant radio announcements updating the villagers about the status of the war dampened Peter's happiness about his recovery. Victory did not follow victory.

In the summer of 1940, news came of the great victory over France and the imminent fall of Britain. Despite his discomfort about the situation, he believed victory was achievable. In May of 1941, he heard the news that Italy, Hungary, Romania, and Germany were now fighting against Yugoslavia, a southern neighbour. He disliked the fact that there was no real reason for a war there because they supported Germany before, but he heard that the young King Peter of Yugoslavia[26] disagreed with the troop movement through his country. Although Peter did not publically say so, he disagreed with this turn of events. In another lifetime, he recalls, he would have said something, but the new arrivals in the village had long since made certain that no one voiced differing views.

Over the past months, men from Germany came in to Heidendorf to talk to the young adults[27]. They wanted to know what each man thought about Germany and about Hitler. He would later learn that they were from the Nazi party. Peter said he did not care one way or another, and the men told him that he needed to change his feelings because he had young sisters in school, and he was old enough to join the army. Peter despised these men and felt that they should not be here. He had much work to do without their interruptions and interviews. Peter didn't care to know the names of the men; although Hans and Heinrich were names he did overhear and learn. In the evenings, there were new patriotic songs that the young people needed to sing. When these men did not leave the village, Peter felt a growing apprehension about making public statements, and the other villagers felt the same. He did not know how long these men would remain until he heard the new announcement over the radio.

In July 1941, Germany and Russia were officially at war. Peter's initial reaction was to curse and kick the nearest pail. He heard about Hungary and Italy declaring war on Russia as well. He disapproved of this decision because, even with the allies Germany had, they were greatly outnumbered. He debated with his brother long into the night over the merits of this war. Michael seemed to think this would be an adventure. Peter argued that this war was death to them all; the Russians would kill all Germans. His brother said something to imply that Peter was a coward. Peter recalls he pounded his fist on the table and said that Hungary would fall if Germany lost.

As time went on, he heard about people leaving for a front far from Hungary—to Russia.

The first men to leave Heidendorf were the Hungarians and they took along some of the horses. Then a call came for more horses to be sent. He did not understand why, if Germany and its allies had all of this wonderful machinery, they needed so many horses.

In 1941, Heidendorf faced the coldest winter that almost anyone could recall. Peter was never so glad that his family's house was not made entirely of wood. The exterior walls were constructed of mortar and stones gathered from the area surrounding the village. He prayed that this coming year would be good and that news of victories at the Russian front might mean that the people who left would come home, and that he would not need to go to Russia. He heard about operational delays and freezing weather in Russia, and he wondered what possessed an army to try to continue fighting during such cold months. He recalls that each night in his prayers, he demanded that God stop this war, but he did not think that this would happen.

The difficulties that Peter and his village faced multiplied before he celebrated his twenty-first birthday in the early months of 1942. He knew that soon he would have to report to the army office in Bistritz and receive his uniform, and then he would wait for a telegram telling him the dates when he must attend training. Although it was his duty to serve in the army, he did not want to leave Heidendorf for Russia. No matter what the men from Germany told them, that they would not need to fight in Russia, Peter believed that he would still end up there. He believed that he would die.

He wanted to be able to have some more education so that when this land was his, it would produce better.

He brooded over the radio announcements about the war. The announcer often proclaimed that victory was at hand, but really, it never was. Peter noticed that there was little mention of loss of life or equipment, in the German Army at least. Peter spoke to his father who told him the one thing that stood out in his memory of the previous war, the Great War, was that according to the news announcers, every victory was great and every defeat small. Peter did not want to ask more questions, fearing the answers. It was not until his father talked to him about going away to work in Berlin that Peter's frustrations exploded. He did not think that his father needed to leave Heidendorf at all and the reason for leaving to go so far away seemed feeble to him.

Money became a concern as Peter's three youngest sisters neared confirmation age. His sister Maria would be confirmed this year and the family needed to pay for material to create her special dress, the Tracht. His parents, his father in particular, tried to explain this to him. Peter argued with his father that his older sister Anna had helped pay for the material for her own dress by going to one of the larger cities to be a housemaid. Maria was perfectly responsible, she could do the same thing, and the money would be of use to everyone. This time his father refused to allow it. Peter almost yelled when he told them he did not see why not. Then his father mentioned that Germany needed some older men to help in their workforces. The money would be much better and his family would have enough to eat and to pay their taxes and for anything else that they might require.

Peter kept his peace because he thought his father would not listen to him anyways. He thought that it would be best for his father to find work in Bistritz so that he could be closer to his family. He worried about his mother, and knew that it would hurt her to see her husband leave. He also wondered if his father was leaving for other reasons. Peter found out much later that his father hoped to use the extra money to pay the Nazis to keep his sons away from the front lines. The worry of serving grew stronger each night in Peter's nightmares.

Peter was miserable when he received his telegram. He knew that it meant his service in the army was required – in his mind it was far too soon. Although he was not sure where he would go exactly (the telegram did not say), he heard that some of the divisions of the Hungarian army were heading for Russia. He recalls that once the news came that men were going there, the mood became more sombre in the village. It was the feeling of waiting to die. He wondered who might be the first man in the village to be killed in action. He prayed that it would not be him. He contemplated what he could do to improve his chances of coming home alive. There were not many options so he dismissed those thoughts from his mind.

Waiting for his telegrams' arrival, coupled with the news that the Russian forces gained decisive victories, made him increasingly agitated. The radio announcer was quick to assure listeners that these victories were not decisive, but Peter looked at the papers that listed the casualties by name, and he found a different story in their pages. Some of the men in the village preferred to believe the announcements on the radio, but Peter recalls that he listened to his uncles and father talk about a similar situation developing at the end of the First World War.

Listening to their stories was of value to him, to a point, but this time the results seemed different. He felt that it was perhaps better because Germany was having more success.

Waiting made him nervous. In reality, although he did not admit it to anyone, it made him afraid. Soon the day came when he received his telegram, and it was an order for him to report to the training grounds when asked; there was no date on it that helped him know when he needed to leave. He hoped it would not be soon, but he knew from what his brother-in-law told him that the order to leave might come the next day.

He waited impatiently and tried to ignore the feelings of fear and frustration he had. He tried to hide the fact that he did not want to lose his life in Russia. He hated the army and the fact he would leave his beloved home, but duty came first. For all that he might want things to be different, duty came first. He was not bitter about it. He resigned himself to serving the needs of the army and the needs of the village. He detested the fact that his younger brother seemed so excited about the chance to join the army, and Peter truly could not understand why he would want to do this. Peter refused to tell anyone about his many fears. He told people that he was waiting for the telegram – nothing more. He did not mention he did not want to go because he was not a coward, and he did not want others to think of him that way. He waited.

In early autumn, the telegram came with instructions that he should go to Bistritz, and he would receive his uniform there. He would begin training and then be sent on to where he was needed. He feared this meant Russia where the fighting and losses grew worse; Hungary and Germany were suffering many casualties. He did not see the point of dying in Russia and vowed that he would survive. He only mentioned his fears to his father and brother-in-law because he trusted that they would not say anything to anyone else. He knew that there could always be someone listening in on private conversations. If someone said something, anything, to those prying men from Germany, he might find himself somewhere worse than Russia. He waited. The waiting was hard, but it gave him time to accomplish more farm work. He felt he needed to work harder while he waited. The harvest came quickly and he helped where people needed him, and he was happy that he could still help. He found other things to accomplish when there were small breaks.

He breathed the fresh mountain air in deep, rhythmic breaths. He looked beyond the emerald hills surrounding Heidendorf to the towering mountains across which he knew he must soon travel. He recalls feeling that he was saying goodbye to the village he loved. He was convinced he would die. Countless men poured into the front in Russia and nameless numbers died. Some of those men were from Heidendorf. Peter prayed that he would one day see his family again, and live. Soon another telegram came with the orders for him to depart Heidendorf after Christmas but no later than March.

He told his parents and siblings that the telegram had arrived. Michael's response was the most startling, he wanted Peter to come back and fulfill his dreams. The family knew that Peter wanted to come back and farm the land, but Peter never felt that this was a dream—rather it was a duty. He also could not understand what excited his brother about the army. He did not learn until later that Michael had only wanted to join the army to make money to further his education. He decided to lay the subject to rest. He still wanted to enjoy this last Christmas together with his family.

It was a silent Christmas. Each person seemed to be deep in thought. Russia loomed large, and Peter believed everyone was wishing him a final farewell. So many young men from Heidendorf who had already left for the front and some of those men were already dead, injured or missing in action. Peter reminded his mother that the midwife told her that he was born healthy and strong, and his mother smiled as if to humour him. He sat for hours in the wooden chair he loved in front of the fire and listened to his father sing. He loved his father's voice, and he wished that one day he would come back and sing with him. He asked his father what to do to stay alive, and the response startled him. Obey the orders you are given and do not ever disobey your commanding officers. Think carefully and be resourceful at the same time. Although he asked, other people did not give him any advice.

Peter noticed that the Nazi party men did not give him any problems. He knew that it was because he was leaving to serve in the army in Russia, which was precisely what they needed him to do. He was now a loyal son of the German Reich. He knew that they did not care if he died.

Peter believed that they were cowards because for all of their grand talk, they were not the ones going to the front lines. He worried about death, but now what he feared more was that he might lose an arm or a leg and he would be useless as a farmer if he returned home injured. He wanted to come home and find a nice woman with whom to share the rest of his life. She would likely be younger than he was, but he did not mind. He thought about Russia and prepared for the trip there.

At the end of October, he travelled to Bistritz. There was a fair held then – a carnival that the Saxons held each year to celebrate the harvest. He received a uniform, and the symbols on it disturbed him. There were a skull and bones in the shape of an X below them. He felt that these symbols marked him for death. No matter how he felt, he knew he had to accept this uniform. He wore it to please his parents, but it was stiff and uncomfortable. They wanted to see their son in the uniform. His mother's reaction came as no surprise. His mother was upset when he wore it because it meant that he was going to leave, but Peter told her that he had no choice; service to his country was his duty. He was trying hard not to let his voice break when he told her that he would be back in Heidendorf in two years. He hoped that with the minimal training he received when he received his uniform, he would be safe. He worried about his brother, though, because Michael seemed preoccupied.

Peter focused his attention on his own departure until the day Michael walked into the house wearing a uniform of his own. He demanded to know why his brother would even consider wearing such a thing. Michael told him that he was joining the cavalry, at the suggestion of friends. Peter demanded more information in an attempt to call his bluff. Michael replied it was Heinrich, one of the German men that Peter so despised, who convinced him, and this was not a joke. This was a temporary situation, Michael explained. The Germans recruited the young boys of Heidendorf to stay in the village and help with marching and taking care of other small tasks so that the older and more experienced men could help the Reich. They needed that experience to wage war against the communist foes of Russia. Michael was not going to go anywhere. Peter yelled at Michael, asking him why he would possibly believe such foolishness from those men. Peter's only hope was that Michael, being as young as he was, would not leave for a fighting front before his return. To his amazement and despair, Michael told him he could not wait to go and do his duty. Peter asked him what duty Michael was imagining, for Peter knew of no duty except for serving and dying and obeying.

Michael told him that the world did not revolve around doing a duty that was not his, but someone else's that he felt he had to do. He should do this because he wanted to serve their country. Peter retorted that duty was duty, and that if it helped others, so much the better. Michael began to get mad, and Peter recalls that his eyes flashed with a rage that he never knew his brother possessed. Michael told him frankly that he had his own dreams and that the army promised that he would fulfill them[28]. Peter did not know how to reply. This was just as well since Michael had already stormed out of the room, closing the door with a thud. Peter recalls that Michael's words haunted him for weeks.

After a few days, Michael acted as if nothing happened but Peter remembers that even his mother pointed out that there was tension between the two of them. Peter was hurt and upset, and he did not hurry to repair the relationship. He wanted Michael to apologize for his stupidity first. Later, he learned that Michael felt the same way.

There was not much to do while he waited for the next telegram. The days were filled mostly with boredom, he did not want to speak to anyone, least of all his brother, and he did not want to go out much in public. He also avoided the family in hopes that no one would point out the state of tension between him and Michael. He spent time reading the Bible; his plan was to read it all before he left, though he did not succeed. This Bible was his mother's, and his grandmother's before that, so he knew he could not take it along to Russia. His mother offered it to him; perhaps she thought that if he took it with him he would return to them safe. It was her way of telling him to come back alive. He declined to take it.

The next time he wanted to do anything was the day when he left for Bistritz. When he arrived, they asked his name, wrote it down, and handed him a gun and knives. The gun came with him on the train. Everyone yelled and screamed orders and the smoke from the train caused him to cough and gag. The wooden railway platform creaked and groaned beneath the booted feet of hundreds of men, each one moving to his assigned place on the train. Peter was ordered into one of the cars. He felt fortunate that he had already completed some training the year before, but that good feeling faded when he found out that this counted as his initial training and service. He boarded a train which initially headed eastward – to Russia. He was certain that the train would stop and he would die shortly thereafter[29].

He kept repeating, in his mind, the midwife's comments at his birth: strong and healthy and a survivor. Somewhere in his journey he headed westward, and between Bistritz and Berlin, he began planning his life after the war. He would survive. He would come home from Russia. He would work in Heidendorf and be a farmer. He would marry and become a father. For that, he just needed to obey orders and survive. He comforted himself with the knowledge that his life was in the hands of God, and he lived when he should have died. He should have died once at the age of six from diphtheria, and again two years ago when he fell ill with typhoid. Perhaps it was fate or a guardian angel. Besides, he had a covenant with his dead sister that he was going to live for both of them, and the thought came to him that she might be protecting him. He hoped so.

The train came to a slow stop and Peter found himself in Berlin, the heart of the new German Reich. He hoped to see his father soon, since he knew that his father planned to come and work there. His father had insisted on leaving the family, and he became more adamant about going away after speaking with the men from Germany though he never told Peter why. His father left before Peter did.

Peter met his father in Berlin,[30] but they did not talk about anything that they should have, only about events in Heidendorf. Peter was offended that his father was working as a lowly security guard, but he recalls that he mollified when his father reminded him it was to provide more money for the family. He did not ask his father what his mother thought of their absence, but he imagined she was upset. In fact, he knew she was because he heard her weep at night and pray for the health of her son. To compensate, she knitted him several scarves, which he took with him.

He tried to think of something positive to call his service in the army, and it was an adventure, after a fashion. With his new adventure ahead of him, Peter worried about the temperature, and he was glad he had packed the scarves. He sometimes wore them under the neckline: white, black, and woollen. Berlin was lovely, and Peter wished that he did not need to leave for the Eastern front. He recalls that he believed that the war might end before he left Berlin – he would only come to the realization many years later that this war was not going to end like the Great War, with Germany's surrender. Hitler would never do such a thing. It did not end. Far too soon, he left the heart of the Reich, and he travelled beyond its borders toward Russia. He always though he would go to Russia, but instead his company received word that they were going northwest of Russia, to Finland.

Since it was close to Russia's borders, Peter expected Finland to be similar to Russia, a vast frozen wasteland, but to his chagrin, he found that it was full of islands and lakes that made the area impossible to defend with any care. He was assigned to the kitchen to work with the food and to gather supplies for the men who were in the panzer divisions. At any other time, he would never come here. There seemed to be no farms and few people. The main city was smaller than Berlin but not much larger than Budapest. He also detested the fact that the place seemed to have no history. It had been a part of the Russian Empire until 1917, but he could see no large buildings. There were only forests and lakes all around, and enemy tanks could be hiding anywhere. He recalls that the only reason he tried not to hate the place was because he believed that the people here were in a similar position as the Saxons; they had to fight or be destroyed by Russia.

For the most part, he found the place bearable. It was not as cold as he expected. It was nearing April, and the ice was slow to melt, but he could see it dripping off the tents, tanks, and other artillery machines in the afternoon sun. The nights were still cold – colder than he had ever thought possible, and this time he was not in a house but in a khaki tent. He cared for the horses that the company had. He fed them, brushed their hair, and kept their enclosure tidy. If it got too cold, he would help with placing tarps over the area. The horses needed protection, too. In fact, he remembers thinking bitterly that the horses sometimes received better care than the men did. As with everything else – equipment and supplies that they had needed to be easily taken down and put up – even the horse enclosure was made of wood that Peter would never use for that purpose in Heidendorf.

He thought of Heidendorf a lot these days, and he wondered how his mother was faring with the farming and having only Michael and his younger sisters to help her. He also agonized over the fate of his brother-in-law Johann, who might receive his orders to leave for the army any day. He was pleased to receive letters from his mother and father. The scrap paper he replied on was harder to write with, but he found time to write. This was not his primary concern, though. His commanding officers needed him to collect packages from the main rail line and to take letters and orders back to the camp. On one of these assignments, if his sense of direction and logic had not been sharp, he would have died.

That day, he went with several men from the company with orders to go and fetch supplies from the railway and to receive reports from Berlin. At the station, they loaded up the wagon and placed some of the bags on the horses, and then they began their return trek to the camp. On their way back, Peter noted that there were more tracks and wheel marks now than when they left. As they continued down the path, he saw more horse tracks. He decided that someone ought to go on ahead and find out what happened. They discussed their options briefly, and they agreed that Peter was the one who should go. He told the others to find a good place to hide, either in bushes or a cave, and he would come back by the evening. If he did not come back by that time, they were to head back to the railway station and wait there – either for him to return or until they received further orders. Then he unloaded one of the horses, mounted, and began to make his way closer to the camp. The only bag he took with him was the bag of reports because they were too vital to leave anywhere. He recalls how responsible he felt about them.

He did not like the fact that the tracks quickly grew more numerous as he closed in on the camp. And when he arrived, everything was gone; all that remained were tent poles and left-over pots and pans. There were no bullets or artillery machines or tanks left, so Peter reasoned that while they had packed up quickly, they did not need to leave anything important behind. He tied his horse to a nearby tree and began to think.

From the camp position, they could have gone in three directions: South would mean heading towards the coast and Berlin, to the West was farther into Finland, towards the neutral country of Sweden, and the last option was east towards Russia. He did not think that they retreated since the company would have passed by him before he got to the deserted camp. A more northerly route would put the company right against the water, and this would be the worst position to be in strategically: Deeper into Finnish controlled territory, or closer to Russia. There was no artillery noise, so he reasoned that they were not in a battle, and if they were, they would have gone west, to get into neutral territory. Moreover, the tracks did not seem to go that way. He decided to head in a more easterly direction. He chose correctly. After about a half hour of riding, he found the company.

He saw his commanding officer and saluted him before handing over the reports. He was relieved that he did not have the responsibility of caring for the packages anymore. If the enemy captured him with those documents, they might interrogate him, thinking he knew more. Then his commanding officer said to the man standing beside him that this soldier could find anything anywhere. Peter noticed that the other man was the superior officer of his commander. The compliment pleased Peter, and he stood a bit straighter, although he did not smile. This was high praise, and Peter wrote about it to his mother.

He was glad to find out that, later in the year, the company would head closer to Heidendorf. He was leaving Russia. He allowed himself a faint hope that he was going home, but he knew in his heart that this would not be the case. The army needed the men in his company elsewhere.

The men boarded train after train, and Peter began to tire of the constant clacking noise. He had more time to think about his family, and he heard that his brother was now a part of the army and could leave home at anytime. He was not sure how his mother was feeling since he knew that she did not like him leaving, and he believed that his brother was leaving with the mindset that this was more of an adventure. Peter had long since stopped thinking of his service as an adventure, and he wondered what his brother thought of war now. He hated the sound of machine gunfire, and he prayed each night that he would survive. He did not like trains for another reason; they made his uniform wrinkled and stained. Even though it did not matter all that much and most of the other men's uniforms were wrinkled and dirty, too, he hated it. It made him long for the days when his mother made sure his clothes were perfect with not a stain or a wrinkle, and in his mind he could hear her sigh when he did get wrinkles on his good clothes. For now, he did not have any reason to keep the uniform neat. Besides, there was no means by which to do so.

The men finished their journey and Peter found himself in the Kingdom of Yugoslavia, fighting the Yugoslavian partisans[31]. He did not understand why these people were fighting in the first place since they had their own kingdom and had supported Germany before. He supposed they wanted something that the German government did not allow them to have. Whatever the reason was, he never had much time to think about it. He needed to be careful. There were snipers to look out for; some would hide themselves in trees, and others would bury themselves in mounds of dirt. Many soldiers were injured or killed by men they never saw. Peter found it a dishonourable means of warfare, but he knew that the German army had snipers too.

He heard from his mother that another death had happened in the family, and that his sister Anna was doing as best she could. Although his mother never told him the exact reason why Anna needed to be strong, he reasoned that perhaps Johann was injured. He hoped that this was all it was, yet he recalls the feeling that somehow he knew that Johann was dead. Since he could only write back to his parents to find out the situation, he did just that. All he could do was wait for their answer and be careful.

Dates in war did not apply to people like him. He was a nameless person, a number in a file. If he died, he would be a number in a different file. He did not want to be important, but he wanted to be missed. In an attempt to mark the passage of time, he devised a way to make dates stay in his mind. The letters that went back and forth between him and his family were a good reference. He marked off the times when he went to Berlin, went to Finland, left Finland, boarded a train. His mother dated her letters and she would mark out pages, using a date or a time as well, though the letters were often only a page long. Now that he was gone for such a long time, he missed his life in the village and his family. He wanted to know about events going on in Heidendorf, but his mother never mentioned them. She only told him who was leaving for war, who was injured, and who had died – all except for two men.

When he found time, Peter flipped back through some of the letters and noticed that his mother did not write about his brother-in-law anymore. Now, he understood why. Johann was dead. He grieved over his death, and Peter thought fondly that he could never remember a time when his brother-in-law was not there to help the family. Johann's death brought back memories of another death – that of his sister.

His past anger at God grew stronger. The best were taken away young, and for some reason he had escaped physical harm thus far. He did not want to die, and he wondered how he could be a better person to honour the memory of those who died young. He realized that even though he was twenty-three – soon to be twenty-four – he had travelled more in the past year than he had in his entire lifetime. He still wanted to learn, to be educated, and maybe one day he would, but that would be, he recalls with bitterness, based upon God's will.

He decided that once he returned to Heidendorf, he would travel no farther from there than Bistritz. He wanted to farm his land, the land that he would receive when his father died, and the land he would give to his eldest son. His responsibility now also extended to his eldest nephew. He needed to teach his nephew little Johann the art of farming now since his father was killed by a sniper's bullet. He spent time writing to his mother, but he noticed that these days he found it harder to write, or harder to find time to write.

This part of Yugoslavia had a similar landscape, vegetation, and climate to Heidendorf, but he wanted to go home now more than ever. He wanted the war to end soon. It was nearly 1945. The thought of deserting his comrades never crossed his mind, and since he was young, duty and honour were paramount in his life. To leave would be dishonourable. Still, he prayed that he would see his family soon. He found that he had an independent spirit within him.

He heard from some men from Transylvania, fellow soldiers, that in September most of Northern Transylvania was ordered to evacuate to a safer area. At first, he thought that it meant all of the Hungarians, Germans[32], and Romanians, but then he realized it meant just the German speakers – which included the Saxons. He could not send letters directly to his family and could not find out where they might have gone or if anyone else was hurt or killed. Also, in the last few months, he could not simply give a letter to his commanding officer and trust that it would arrive. Now he needed to forward it through the command center, and this meant that his letters were screened. He knew this happened because sometimes some of the letters he received from his family asked him about things he wrote about before. He was careful not to write anything negative regarding the war.

In 1945, he was still in Yugoslavia. He still did not receive much news from his parents, though he knew that from their letters that they and his sisters were safe. He suspected that someone else in the family had died because his mother no longer mentioned Michael when she wrote to him. He waited for another letter to see if his suspicions were correct. His parents still believed that Michael had somehow survived the siege of Budapest, but Peter heard reports from survivors that anyone who was caught by the Russians there was killed and mutilated beyond recognition. Michael's cavalry unit had a large number of Saxons in it, and that unit was decimated and its few survivors joined with other groups during that siege.

In his own fashion, Peter mourned for Michael. He was not as close to his brother as he would have liked because their personalities and age difference made it hard. Perhaps it was because of the terse words that they had exchanged, possibly because of something more. In the last while that Peter was in Heidendorf, they had grown closer, but they had never apologized for the last fight. He now felt that he needed to find a way to remember Michael and to carry on with his own life. Peter wanted to be with his family even more since now his mother and father would grieve over both Michael and their elder daughter Sofia who died in 1927. He needed to survive; he was the last of their sons. He hated the mud, the guns, the tanks, the planes, the screams, the cries, and the yells of the injured and dying men. He hated the sight of bodies with cloths over them being carried or dragged away. The dead were buried in unmarked mass graves. He began to believe that this war would never end.

When the war finally did end, Peter found himself not heading home but to a prisoner of war camp in Yugoslavia. Freedom was the only thing in his mind. He did not know when he would be free, or if he would ever possibly be a free man. He wanted to see his family and grow old, but barbed wire and sentries stood in his path. The food was good, and he was thankful that he had enough to eat. He received letters from his family who had left Transylvania in the fall of 1944. Now they were living on the border of Germany and Austria at an Austrian address. After conversations with other men, he discovered that since his parents no longer resided in Romania the Yugoslavian army would not release him because they feared he would go back to Germany. If he lived in Romania or Hungary, they might release him earlier. He waited. How long he needed to wait, no one would tell him.

He put the languages that he learned in the village school to good use. There was a man from Hungary, a fellow prisoner, who spoke Yugoslavian and Romanian. Since Peter could speak Romanian, they became friends. The man knew the general area where Peter once lived, and he took it upon himself to explain to the guards that Peter was not a citizen of either Austria or Germany, but of Hungary and Romania. This meant that Peter could go free earlier. The only problem was that since his parents now had an Austrian address, he could not prove he had lived in Romania. After the administration considered this, they informed Peter that he had permission to leave the camp to return home – to Romania[33].

He agreed.

Peter recalls the day he left the camp. The guards gave him a train ticket to the border of Romania and Yugoslavia. From the border of Romania he could make his own way home. He did not mind. He was not going alone. One of his friends from a nearby Saxon village travelled with him. Together they boarded the train bound for Romania. They transferred to another train bound for Bistritz, but the train did not get that far. At the end of the War, the retreating German army had blown up as many bridges as they could. They would have to walk.

One hundred and sixty kilometres is a long walk, but Peter did not comprehend how long until he walked that distance through the mountains of Transylvania. His army boots were still in decent condition, and for this he was grateful. They walked at a leisurely pace, and it was, for the most part, the easiest thing about their journey. Peter worried about the other parts. He secretly hoped the bridge across one of the larger rivers was still intact. Despite all the years of living near a creek, Peter never learned how to swim, and he knew that a standard tactic of retreating armies was blowing up any bridges that they came across.

They arrived and found that the bridge was in pieces, and Peter recalls that he sank to his knees in despair. Huge chunks of concrete and wood were all that remained. The river, swollen and angry, rushed past the broken blocks and wood planks. Peter and his friend discussed their plan. They decided to swim across.

Peter had his doubts, but his friend instructed him that no matter what, he needed to keep his head up and his arms and feet moving. Keep moving. Peter did exactly that. The water rushed past him and although it was not winter, the water froze his hands and feet. He kept his head up and his arms and legs moving. He reached the far edge of the river and pulled himself out. The cold water made his legs go numb and he doubted that he could continue walking. He began to shiver, and he wished he had a brandy to warm himself up. He was glad that his friend suggested they build a fire. Once they were warm and dry, they continued walking.

They walked to Bistritz. There, Peter met a cousin who had stayed behind. She told him that his family was safe. He could not leave Romania yet, but he hoped to join them in their new home soon. As much as he wanted to return to Heidendorf, she told him that the Romanians now owned everything. He would have nothing, not even a home.

This time when Germany lost the war, the Saxon people lost their homeland and traditions. The homes were gone and the people were evacuated or sent to Russian labour camps. Many did not return to Transylvania. If they did come back, they faced The same situation that Peter faced. Instead of going back to Heidendorf, he made the decision to stay in Bistritz. And it was there that he met his beloved wife, his darling Sofia.

Sofia lived in Bistritz as well and she came from a small village like the one he had come from. She was working as a housecleaner for a local lawyer, and he worked as a labourer. They met and decided to marry shortly after that. It seemed like a simple idea except that after the war it was illegal for two Germans to marry in Romania. Peter, ever resourceful and very much in love, recalls that he found a way. In a discussion with the lawyer, Peter and Sofia found that if they had the proper legal documents they could be married but not in a Lutheran Church. They decided to exchange their vows in the lawyer's office. He wrote to his family to tell them the good news. He was sad that he could not give his new wife Sofia a proper wedding in a church, but this was the only way that they could accomplish it at the time, and he wanted to marry her as soon as possible.

They did not plan to leave Romania, but bureaucracy once again took over. Peter and Sofia were called to the main city office where one of the officials told Peter that since he was a German who served in the war, he would have twenty-four hours to leave Romania. The official tried to torment Peter by calling him a Nazi. It was thanks to the support of his wife, and his own self-control that Peter did not shout. Afterwards, he told his cousin about the meeting and his cousin helped them board a wagon. She drove with him and Sofia as close to the

border as possible and, after wishing them well and a safe journey, the cousin left.

Peter and Sofia walked towards Germany and his family. It
took them seven weeks, and they often slept beneath the stars
or inside warm barns. One evening it rained and they found
shelter under sunflowers; they were not wet in the morning.
When they reached their destination, his family welcomed them.
Peter was glad that his mother welcomed Sofia as a daughter.
Even though he knew that it was a part of their tradition that
a daughter-in-law becomes a part of the family, this still pleased
him. He worried that since they did not live in Heidendorf anymore that the village's traditions would die out.

Sofia and Peter remained in Germany for the next eight
years. His father, mother and sisters and his niece and nephews
left for Canada in 1950.

Peter thought that he and Sofia would stay in Germany forever, but his plans changed again. His father wrote to his sister, Peter's aunt Maria, who lived in Germany. He implied in
his letters that his son being so far away was causing him pain.
With a hint of bitterness, Peter decided that duty to his father
and family – his extended family – came first, and he and Sofia
decided to go to Canada. This time it was not only him and
Sofia moving to a new place but also their two young sons –
Young Peter and Philip.

They never had any daughters, but Peter knew that if they
had, the eldest would be named Sofia, after his wife and his sister who died young. He carried on the tradition of the Saxons
and named his eldest son after himself. His many attempts at
instilling other traditions of the Saxons in his sons had mixed
results. These mixed results also carried on to his children and
great-grandchildren. He is proud of them, and once he arrived
in Canada they were able to settle in an area with many Saxon
people.

He wonders what life would be like in Transylvania. Not as
good as this life here, I respond. He laughs and says, no not as

good. He looks out of the window, and tells me that I should read more books. I ask him which ones I should read. Perhaps something on farming or winemaking, he muses. I ask him if there is anything that he misses.

He glances my way, and he thinks for a moment.

He misses her of course. After sixty years of having his beloved by his side, he misses her. The chance to farm in Germany, perhaps, but a great life in Canada certainly made up for it. The next generations, the grandchildren and great-grand-children, they live far away now. I ask him, is there anything you would change in your life?

He looks at the picture of him and his wife, and he smiles. I know his answer. I know better than to say much to him. He would never hear me. His is thinking of two ladies that he loves, and two men that he misses, and the fact he is still alive to tell me his true story.

A Requiem for Lies

Peter can only imagine what Michael is thinking, but it would have been the same as he is; Budapest was the lie of all lies. Michael did not write this to anyone, and would not want to either... he had wanted to join the army after all. He did not want to write, and in reality, he could not take time to do so since the bombs and the snipers would kill him if he stopped even for a moment. He knew he was dead anyways. His job, whatever that meant, was to keep the horses calm, and it was not an easy task.

He would wake up at all hours and dream about an education, a farm, a life. He had none of that, and Budapest was a mess, grey and deadly. It felt like a tomb. No, he could not write, and would not write. He did not want to admit that he had made a mistake believing in the lie, and having to tell Peter that he was right – that would be the worst.

The calls ring out and he and his friend saddle the horses to make an escape, maybe to get back home alive, and safe. He needs to drag the frightened horse out of the tent that they made for it. Bombs are exploding close to them. He gets on the horse and gallops westward; the bombs and the Russian army have different plans. Still, he urges the horse to go faster. Behind him are the sounds of Russian tanks, coming closer by the second...

He was the prankster, the joker, the precocious younger son, and that is how his sisters and brother remember him. They examine a photo taken of the family in 1942. All of them were so young and full of dreams. They each have their own thoughts about his life, many of them bittersweet. They all agree that

Michael was the personification of joy, someone who valued life, and he attempted everything with gusto. His siblings are old now, and his brother muses that soon he will be joining Michael in heaven. He likens it to a reunion of sorts, and maybe there will be a bit of forgiveness. As he thinks of that reunion, he smiles and laughs before saying that his mother is probably chasing Michael up there with a broom. His sisters all break into peals of laughter, appreciating this reminder of his antics, and it brings him back to life in their hearts.

Being born a few days after 1 April 1924, his emerging personality should have come as no surprise. He loved to make people laugh; he loved pranks and kind-hearted jokes. The planting season was underway, and Michael joined the family with perfect timing; his mother went into labour after everyone had left for the day. He also had the distinction of being both the smallest and loudest of the children born thus far.

He received the sacrament of holy baptism in the Lutheran Church at four weeks of age. His father chose the name Michael to honour the memory of his younger brother who had died in the First World War while serving in Italy[34]. At his baptism Michael was the only one of his siblings to cry through the whole service. His sister Anna and his brother Peter remember his baptism more for the celebration afterwards than the service itself because for them it meant dining on corn, ham, and cake. They remember singing and wine, and Anna remembers that she was allowed to hold the baby provided she did not move at all. Michael was an energetic baby, and he promptly began to cry out and wiggle.

The years passed quickly and Michael was brought up with the same values as his older siblings. By the age of three, he was well versed in what a responsible boy should learn and how he should act. In January of 1927, his younger sister Maria was born. Michael was excited for the birth, but also felt sad because he realized he was no longer the youngest in the family, and his sister Anna recalls he was a bit sad and cried out for his mother. As he spent more time with Maria, he learned to love her and she brought happiness to the family. His sister Anna remembers that Michael would always give Maria a good night kiss and help his mother place her in the cradle.

In the summer, Michael and his older siblings Peter, Anna, and Sofia all caught colds. It soon became apparent to their parents that their children were suffering from the contagious disease diphtheria. The fever and the swelling of Michael's neck confirmed their suspicions and he and his siblings were quarantined in their house. His parents and Maria relocated to his grandmother's to avoid contagion. His aunts helped in the home, but to Michael, they were no replacement for his mother. His brother Peter remembers how he would yell for his mother until he was exhausted. His sister Sofia died after a struggle to breathe, and she was buried shortly afterwards.

Michael did not understand the concept of death and kept asking why she was not coming back to see him. Once he had regained his health and was reunited with his parents, he clung to his mother looking for answers. It was somewhat fortunate that since he was so young the memory of his sister's passing dimmed with time and he wasn't haunted by the loss in the same way as Anna, Peter and his parents[35].

In a culture that was somewhat closed to discussions about personal feelings, Michael acted out these feelings by being the prankster of the family. The jokes and pranks were mostly harmless. His sister Katharina remembers that he once pretended that he scared the chickens and that they were all running loose in the garden. When his mother discovered that the chickens were fine, she started to laugh and threatened to chase him with the broom. Michael of course did it again, only this time he put a chicken into the garden. Katharina remembers she only saw Michael sprinting out of the house with his mother in pursuit, broom in hand. He took full advantage of the fact that he was the younger brother, and his parents had fewer expectations of him.

He might have wished for another brother, but his mother gave birth to two more sisters Katharina and Sofia after 1927. He found a playmate in his sister Katharina, and Sofia remembers that Katharina and Michael were the most boisterous in the family. He enjoyed the time he spent with his elder siblings, too. They in turn remember that Michael was always talking about being with them. Michael always wanted to be with them, even in school.

He hoped to spend more time with his older brother and older sister once he started school. He told his brother Peter that he looked forward to the adventures school would give him. Peter recalls that Michael was angry when he told him that school was not a big adventure. His sister Anna remembers that Michael was excited when his mother gave him schoolbooks and a chalkboard and chalk out of the chest by her bed.

What he imagined about school was different from reality. Anna remembers how he complained that although they sat together in straight rows of desks, no one was allowed to speak unless the teacher spoke to them. The teacher often compared Michael to his older brother. Since Michael was more boisterous than his brother was, the comparisons were often negative[36]. He never learned to like writing letters or tests, but he worked hard and succeeded with good grades. His dream of getting a further education than the seven years the village school offered was always in the back of his mind. He did not dream of fame or fortune, although he wanted some money as well. Heidendorf was a farming village and it required knowledgeable, caring farmers. His dream was to help the villagers produce better crops and stronger livestock, and this required further education.

In January of 1937, the family celebrated the wedding of Michael's sister Anna. He liked his new brother-in-law. Johann was fourteen years older than Michael was, but seemed to enjoy his company, and Michael would later tell Anna that this pleased him since their personalities were so different. Michael was not confirmed yet so he was not allowed to play a prominent role in the wedding ceremony[37]. The church was full of people on the day of the wedding and it was a solemn occasion. Michael sat with the other boys and unmarried men of the village, remaining quiet. His mind was elsewhere, though, and Sofia remembers that he was one of the first to get to the food table. After the ceremony, there was dancing and singing, lead by his father. During that evening, Michael realized that Anna would no longer be in the house. In one day, the family both grew and shrunk. His sister Sofia remembers that he commented that he was not crying – it was just dust.

He tried not to listen in but he kept overhearing the debate between his father and his brother Peter about the country of Czechoslovakia after Anna's wedding. A man whom he had never heard of, or at least thought he never heard of, signed a peace treaty with Adolf Hitler. His questions about the man's name resulted in a look of despair from his father, and Peter remembers that he saw Michael pouring over books to find his answer; it was Neville Chamberlain, Prime Minister of Great Britain. His parents explained that this treaty prevented a war between Great Britain and Germany. The tension in the village did not lessen. At first, his parents would not tell him more, and he got upset that they would not until he noticed the worry that his father showed. He had never seen his father pray so much or be so silent. One day, his father told him: There would be another fight, perhaps a war.

The Nazis in Germany were trying to regain territory in Poland. The two countries Britain and France—especially France—did not want Germany to have this land back. In September 1939, rumour spread that Germany was attacked by some personnel in the Polish army and took men into Poland. This would later prove to be untrue, but Nazi Germany used that pretext to declare war on Poland. Soon after this declaration, there was a declaration of war on Germany by the three countries of France, Poland, and Britain. That was what

Michael was told, nothing more. Michael knew better than to ask for more information, as his sister Katharina recalls it was a time where he understood the dangers of war.

His father was worried that his sons and son-in-law would die far from the land they loved, exactly like his own brother did in 1917 in Italy. Michael worried, too, that he might die like his namesake uncle, and he expressed his private fears to his sisters.

He also overheard a conversation between his brother and brother-in-law saying that the army paid well and might even allow for some of the village men to further their education in agriculture. Michael wondered if war might not be such a bad thing, and if Germany won, that he might be able to get that education without asking for money from his parents. He knew that he needed to be confirmed in the Lutheran Church and that would happen in the coming spring of 1939. He also knew that war could be dangerous, and men faced death.

Michael believed that the army would help him. He knew from the work Johann did that the army did pay reasonably well and that would make a difference. Since Michael did not have a family, he could save more money. For now, he decided that working hard in the fields and asking questions to the right people would allow him to gain the background knowledge he might need. He hoped that the practical knowledge learned here would help him in school and in the future as well. The planting season was a good time to begin working towards his dream.

He loved to listen to the radio with the other men. Now that he was confirmed, he was allowed to share his opinions, but this did not mean that others would listen to him. His brother often laughed at some of his comments. He asked why Germany would want a war. The answer was, to protect their land and territory from France who wanted to punish Germany. Michael was happy, and so were some of the other men, when they heard that France was defeated and Germany achieved a great victory. He wondered why his brother-in-law continued to fret. Then someone explained that Britain was still in the battle and some people worried that Russia would declare war on Germany. Michael did not think that this would happen. France was defeated, and for now, peace was a reality for the world. The harvest would soon take over his time, and he concentrated on that.

Michael wondered why each evening the men would talk of nothing other than Romania and Hungary. From his school days, he knew that Hungary wanted its former land back, and Transylvania was a part of that. As the end of October neared and with the harvest now finished, the men talked about other events that happened over the year. Some worried about another bad winter followed by poor crops the next year. Others talked about how the soil might be improved so that the effects of that winter would not matter as much. Michael asked if they should not send young men to Bistritz to find more improved methods of farming. They dismissed this idea. Michael was not one to be deterred, and he kept asking how to better the lives of the people in Heidendorf. His brother-in-law often reminded him that not everything could be done within one generation. The conversations, though, always seemed to turn back to events that were out of the control of anyone in the village. These events, though, did have a way of changing lives.

In the summer of 1940, when Michael heard that the northern area of Transylvania was returning to Hungarian rule after over twenty years he was excited, and he smiled and laughed more. He played more jokes and he even danced better. To some people, it was as if Michael had realized a dream. Others thought he was like any other boy enjoying something new and different that excited him. The people close to Michael knew that for him this was a step towards Budapest[38]. It would be less expensive to travel to Budapest now that Heidendorf was located within the borders of Hungary. He spent the winter enjoying the dances and singing. He knew that, come the early part of February, the preparation work to have the planting season begin on time would need to start.

Michael grew taller this year and was now almost the same height as his brother. His mother commented frequently that she had to lengthen his pants and sleeves. He did not mind getting his clothes lengthened since this meant that he might grow taller than Peter. He never liked being smaller than his older brother, recalls his sister Katharina, and he hated the comparisons that people made about his height. He was glad that he was taller than his father, who told him that he would be as tall as his uncle Michael was.

Michael enjoyed the evening gatherings that the villagers of Heidendorf had. Now, though, he saw new faces in the crowd. In a village where everyone knew each other, to have men come in from Germany was interesting. At first, they encouraged the young boys and men to exercise more. They suggested soccer, and Michael found this to be an interesting game with a lot of running. These men wanted the boys to play the game out in the meadows and practice and work together. If it was in the summer, he told his family, he might be more interested in trying to play the game, but it was near the planting season and these strangers did not understand this. Then they began to talk to the men of the village individually. Michael would tell his sisters and brother that they asked what he felt about Germany and being a German. Then they asked more questions.

They also asked him did he want more education or to continue to work on the farm? When Michael told them that he wanted more education so that he could help produce better crops for the village, the men seemed pleased. He mentioned, though, that before he told them the second part of this dreams, about producing better crops, they were not happy and seemed to want to discourage him from further education. The Nazi men also asked him about his feelings towards the German government. Michael told them he did not feel anything either negative or positive. Later he told his family how uncomfortable these men made him feel.

Even the singing in the evenings changed. Although Michael did not mind changes to both the culture of the village and the routines of the day, he was not sure about the new songs that the young adults sang. Some of the music seemed quicker and more determined than the songs he was used to singing. He enjoyed the melodies but not the words. Having grown up in a home that valued church and God above all, some of the words seemed to praise everything German. He also did not understand why the men wanted him to join in Sunday morning marches instead of going to church. He went when one of the men suggested that his father needed to work more. With his father still recovering from typhoid fever, Michael wanted to protect him. He joined the marches and singing on Sundays occasionally.

The visiting men were not happy and told him so, but Michael would tell his mother that he did not like going to the marches or the singing. These newcomers did not uphold the traditions of the Saxons, which he valued so highly. Sofia recalls that he had truly hoped that the Nazis might do so, but they did not. One of the few things that he liked about them was their promise of an education in the city of Budapest, Hungary, but they did not tell him much beyond the promise of that education and a return to the village. He looked forward, knowing that after the planting he would have more time to help with the animals and to avoid the men.

The summer of 1941 passed quickly for Michael. He enjoyed shoeing the horses and grooming and caring for them. It was a lot of work but his uncles always were nearby to lend a hand. Some were better with the horses than others were. He listened to them more and found he had a good ability with the animals. He also found that if he saddled the horse he could often ride it. His brother remembers that after his first ride, he came back with many bumps and bruises, but he was excited to have ridden a horse. His sister Katharina remembers that he joked that he would learn to ride horses and join the carnival.

His mother got upset and told him to stop saying that until she realized that he was joking. After that, she would often tell him to run off to the carnival if that was what he wanted, especially when he did something that made her cross.

That summer brought worrying news to Heidendorf. Michael was not happy to hear that Germany had declared war on Russia and was in the process of invading that country. To him Russia was too large and there was no need to attack them—in fact, he told his brother they were best left alone. He wondered why Germany would do such a thing because they had recently declared war on the Balkan kingdom of Yugoslavia. He heard from his father that this lead Hungary into the war against Yugoslavia. He could not understand why Germany would want to fight a war on two fronts, but he also felt that since Italy and Hungary were also fighting in Yugoslavia, that war would be won soon.

He did not know, since the announcements did not share news of defeats with the German population of Europe, that Italy was a junior partner and did not have the most advanced technology. He knew that there must be defeats since men were already dying. He, his father, his brother, and brother-in-law were told that the might of the German army would crush the Russians, even though the Russians had more men. Michael wondered how this could be possible since the Russians had more mechanized infantry and, more importantly, more soldiers.

Michael heard the rumours of victories and defeats from the radio in the Heidendorf town hall. Most of these news reports were slanted to exaggerate Germany's victories or minimize the defeats in the battles they fought. In the evenings, the men of the village would gather and discuss the day's events. The men would sometimes talk about the war, but he knew no one shared his true feelings. Everything people said outside their family home was carefully thought through first. They all worried, and they knew that they were being watched. He was not sure why the men from Germany, the Nazis, would always promise everyone that the German army would soon crush their opponents. This never happened.

He heard about the losses that the Russians suffered and the great victories the Germans won. His sister remembers that he kept some of his feelings to himself, but he told her he was beginning to think about what might happen if the German Army continued to lose in the battles. He worried about the events that were happening, and he would later tell his older sister that his brother-in-law asked him to help her in any way that he could. He was not sure how he might do that, but he would try. Katharina remembers that she explained to him that her husband might need to leave and she would need help with planting. Michael agreed to help her and to give her as much support as he could.

He believed that he had good understanding of working with animals and the care and feeding of them. He was not interested in fighting with the infantry, but he found out that there would most likely be some cavalry units serving, too. They would bring supplies behind the front line panzers, the mighty tanks of the German Army, and he knew that if he were part of the cavalry that there was a smaller chance that he would need to fight. In a small way, that disappointed him, but he did not want to die without a reason, and the reasons that the men from Germany gave were not good enough for him.

He wanted to do something heroic for the good of his fellow man and not just fellow Germans, as his sister recalls. He spent more time listening to the village men who helped in the stables. He made sure that he knew how to shoe a horse in faster time, and how to feed it so that it would take longer before the horse became hungry again. He knew that a mixture of grass and coarse ground corn with hay often made the horses less hungry. The summer was coming and he knew that he would soon have more time to think and work.

He enjoyed the time that he spent working in the fields, but he also went off with his father to help chop wood. His sister

Sofia recalls that he would often brag about how long it took him to chop down the biggest tree he could find, and then yell that the tree was falling. Of course, he always found that game amusing until his father would tell him someone might get hurt, often suggesting he might be that person. He had done this every year, but this fall of 1941 he wanted to chop more wood, and without any joking about.

Now Michael wanted to cut down smaller trees and get more in for the winter, and if this might be of use for other things that Heidendorf needed, he wanted to be able to do that. He also did other things that seemed more unusual to his nature. He spent time with his niece and infant nephew. He told his sister that he felt he needed to see them more. He did not say why although his sister Anna suspects that he seemed to know that the war was not going well and he would need to leave soon. The family needed his help for the harvest and his father encouraged him to do anything he could. Michael was glad to have this support from his father, and he would admit to his sisters later that it was the only thing he was glad about in a while.

Just before Christmas in 1942, his brother Peter received a telegram informing him that he needed to leave for the army soon. Peter would leave for Russia, and the family felt certain he would die. Michael knew that this meant that his father would need his help more than ever. The harvest came and he wanted to do as much good work as he could. He was eighteen now, and if the war continued to go badly, the Hungarian army might need him to report for duty sooner than the mandatory age of twenty-one. His father told all of his children that by the end of the First World War – his father still called it the Great War – they were calling men as young as eighteen to fight.

Michael worried about this, but he felt that there might be a great victory in store for Germany, and then the people would come home. He noticed that many of his older friends were excited about leaving to serve for glory. He told his sisters and brother that he wondered why anyone would want glory after fighting in such a manner. He soon learnt that the radio announcements were not correct. He would later tell his sisters that if one looked at the number of losses that both armies had, it was not hard to understand why the people were better off not to know things. He later told people that what he felt did not matter; what he did was more important.

Michael still enjoyed telling jokes and playing small pranks. This was his way of making people happy. He did not take pleasure in relaying bad news, and he would try to soften the blow with some sort of joke, or if he knew that a joke was not appropriate, he would find another person to tell the person the bad news. It seemed to his family that Michael could not face sadness when others felt it.

Christmas was good this year because the whole family was still in Heidendorf, but his brother had recently received his telegram telling him that he must depart soon after the holiday. Michael never told anyone exactly how he felt, but most of them remember that he did not say much, only to wish his brother the best in his own manner. He seemed to brood more and to think about what the future might hold for him and his friends and family should the war come closer. He did not mind spending time with his friends; it seemed he relished the idea. He still went to the singing and fellowship events with the other youths of the village, and his younger sisters remembered that he now took more care with his clothes and never seemed to get many stains on them, whereas before he always came back with one or more. He worried about his brother-in-law as well, for although he had served in the Romanian Army once already, he was still young enough to be called to serve in the Hungarian army as well. He did not refer to his worries in daily conversation (at least, none of his siblings recall him doing so), but they are all certain it was on his mind.

Michael still looked at the prospect of joining the army with a mixture of fear and excitement because the men from

Germany promised him that he could remain in Heidendorf if he joined the army. They would not ask him to make the journey to Russia because the war would be over soon; they simply wanted men willing to help show support for Germany. He wanted to return to Heidendorf after he studied agriculture at a school in Budapest to help with producing a better quality crop. His father encouraged him to work hard, to listen, and to follow instructions. Michael later told his sister Maria that it was more for that promise of a further education than for supporting the cause that he decided to join the army. There was no choice. If he wanted to help Heidendorf later and not go to Russia, he would need to be in the army now.

He had photos taken with friends while wearing his new uniform, and learned to his delight that many of them approved of his decision to serve. Many of them were now in uniform as well. By contrast, his mother despaired. She worried that both her sons would leave and not return. His sister Maria remembers that she counted the days until Peter left. She often tried to get the date when Michael would leave from him. He assured her it was a temporary absence. From the tone of his voice, people knew he did not believe it was temporary. By the time his brother left for Russia, he told some people that he did not think that he would go to Russia but would travel south instead. He heard this his destination was Yugoslavia. The fighting was still raging there.

Michael tried to keep the gloom from people. He would joke, laugh, and talk to everyone. Some noticed that he did not seem to be happy or joyful, though. His brother and brother-in-law left for the Eastern front[39] at the end of 1943 and early in 1944. He knew that his brother-in-law did not want to leave, and Michael hoped that he would not be hurt. He spent more time with his sister Anna and his niece and nephew. By the end of the year, Anna told him that she was expecting again. Michael suddenly seemed happier than he had been in a while. He laughed more. He joked more. To Anna it seemed he knew that this baby would be special to all of them, a bit of joy in this uncertain time.

This happiness over the new baby ended far too soon. Anna remembers the dark winter evening in February 1944, when her family learned that Johann was killed while on route to Russia. That evening Michael was with her at her house, and Anna remembers how preoccupied he seemed. He would wander around the house smiling only at the children, and then he would suddenly walk out of the house without a word, only to return a few minutes later appearing as if he had been crying. When she asked him what was wrong he would not tell her; he simply changed the subject.

She observed that, unusual for Michael, who often spent hours talking about the war, he did not refer to it at all that evening. He also refrained from joking, and his eyes seemed haunted by news she could not define. She remembers that when she asked about their brother he smiled a bit and said he was all right. The tension in the small house grew as Michael repeatedly refused to share the information Anna wanted, and she remembers the troubled look on his face. As the evening progressed and Anna put the children to bed, Michael left for a few minutes, longer than before, and then he returned with their aunt, whose face was full of concern. Michael looked into his sisters eyes, kissed her on the cheek, and told her to sleep well and that she was very brave. He got up and left, and then her aunt gently told her that her husband had been killed.

Michael promised to help with the planting, and the winter seemed good. Anna remembers that he told her he would help where he was needed and for as long as possible. By the winter of 1943, the war was going badly for the German army. Michael had to leave before planting was complete. Maria remembers that he seemed distant, as if he knew he would die. He seemed to think that his name was linked to his dead uncle's. He stopped joking and smiling. The radio only announced defeat after defeat.

He was excited that he could finally do something, though. He did not know where he was going, and he hoped to be able to come home soon. He travelled with other troops west. To his delight, he stopped in Budapest. From there his family no longer heard from him; the war was raging, and letters became almost impossible to write or to send.

Budapest was not what Michael expected, Maria believes, and this might have moved him not to write. The siege of Budapest was raging and hundreds of soldiers and civilians died each day. For most of the injured, it was certain death. They were left where they were wounded, and the leaders of the Hungarian and German armies were ordered by Hitler to hold the city and not surrender. Because of this order, thirteen thousand civilians died of their wounds from mines and bombs; twenty-five thousand starved. Budapest was bombed by both sides almost continuously.

Maria and Anna feel that Michael might have survived, but that there was an order for the troops to fight to the bitter end. Given that Michael would likely obey this order, and seeing the senseless deaths, he would not want to admit to them that he had made a potentially fatal error in judgement. Still, they both believe that Michael would have survived somehow.

His brother Peter found a story that differed. From the information he later pieced together, Peter believes Michael made his way with his company to Budapest, and was in the cavalry division[40]. By the end of the war, the battle for Budapest raged and ragtag bands of survivors attempted to free themselves from the death trap that the city had become. The civilians who had remained in the city tried to flee, too. The Germans blew up the eight bridges over the Danube River that divided Buda and Pest to hinder the progress of the Russian troupes.

By February of 1945, with the certain defeat of the Germans in Budapest, the remaining civilians and the forces of the German and Hungarian armies who could leave left. Anyone else was killed or captured as a prisoner of war. Peter later spoke with a soldier who saw a German soldier on horseback going west-ward at full gallop. He called to him asking if there were others, to which the other man replied two others – one of whom was Michael – were behind him and should be coming soon. The German did not stop, did not look back, and kept the horse at full gallop.

The soldier, after waiting for as long as he dared and with no other German soldiers in sight, fled. The bombs shook the earth and he could make out the shapes of the oncoming tanks. Peter feels that with the Russians advancing as fast as they did, his brother was most likely killed or injured. Since there was never further contact, Peter assumed that Michael was dead or died as a prisoner of war. He hopes that he died somewhere on that road, for any man, soldier or civilian, who survived the siege of Budapest was captured and sent to Russia. Many of them were taken to the Russian labour camps, and few ever returned.

A Childlike Hope and
A Man's Gun

He did not want to meet any soldiers, and he certainly did not want to be caught by the Russians. He had heard rumours that they would kill any young German boys on sight. The Americans might do the same. He hoped that his age would be a shield, but he knew it would not be if he were caught. He had had training in the huge tents, and he had heard what had happened to the defeated Germans in Poland and in his own village. He was not a Saxon anymore; he was someone who needed to run and hide. He was a defeated German.

He hated what both sides did in this war. He hated that he had not known, and he hated what was happening now. He needed to find his parents and the rest of his family. He wanted to find them, and he was loath to admit that this might never happen. He was not sure if he would ever see them again. War was nothing like he had imagined, and he wondered about the older boys who feared dying in the war; their deaths might have been the right choice – living with the memories is not easy.

Stephan hates gophers with a passion. They are the bane of his existence, and no matter how cute they might look, they make a mess in his flowers. Of course, now that he is older and does not hunt anymore, he hates them even more. He sits outside in the sun, nursing a beer. He grunts when someone tells him he could stand to lose some weight. His father has a gut, and so does he, but he is still healthy. He will live to be a hundred. He glances my way as if daring me to contradict him. I do not.

He slams his fist on the table, causing the drinks to shake and his wife to glare at him. He booms out, "So, you want a story? I have a story for you. I was young once you know, and don't you dare laugh." He glances my way as if to see if even a small giggle will escape my mouth. "I was a part of a great move; I left my home. It really was not much. I came to Canada and met my wife, and had two yahoos…children." I can tell he only adds the word children after seeing the glare his wife gives him.

His wife points out that they have three children. "I'll get to him," Stephan growls. "Besides, the last yahoo…son, came years later. I worked hard and I hunted, and I still have good aim. Then the last yahoo – child came." He looks at his wife as if to say, are you happy? She shrugs her shoulders and rolls her eyes. She tells me with a laugh that she gave up on him a long time ago. She asks all of us if we would like anything to drink. After listening to our requests, she tells Stephan to be nice and regale people with his story.

His reply is nearly a snort: "It's not just a story; it's true. I did do these things. Now pull up a seat and listen. Don't forget to ask any questions you think up in your head!"

Then he begins.

Senndorf was a small village south of Bistritz, and the people who lived in the village were close and everyone knew one another. More precisely, they knew each other's business very well. Stephan started out his life here. He was born in 1930, in a world at peace, and in a home that longed for a son. His mother gave birth to him in the bedroom of her house with the aid of a midwife. The family marvelled at how black his hair was and how much of it he had. Many of the people who saw Stephan felt he would grow strong since he could cry and make his needs known to those around him. His father was pleased that he now had a son who would carry on the family name and his name as well. Stephan was baptized at four weeks old, and the service was followed by a celebration at the family home.

Once Stephan was old enough to understand collecting eggs from the hens, his mother and grandmother showed him how and explained he should do it very carefully because the hens would not lay eggs if they were disturbed too much. In the morning, he would go to the hen coop and peer into each nest. If a hen was on the nest, he knew not to touch the eggs since there would be new chicks. If a hen was not on the nest and had not been there in a while, he collected those eggs. Sometimes he would wait two days after the hens laid the eggs to make sure that he could collect them. He had to be careful not to move the nest much and not to press to hard on the eggs. Once he had the eggs gathered in a basket, he would give them to his mother; she would wash them and make sure that they were good to eat. By the time he turned five, he could help in the garden pulling the weeds and hoeing. At the age of five, he began school.

His parents' expectations for schoolroom behaviour were clear: he should behave well in the class, and he should do his work with the utmost care. The school he went to was the Senndorf village school. It only had one room and was made of bricks and mortar with large wooden beams supporting the roof. At the one end of the room was a blackboard where the teacher wrote his notes. Stephan found the classroom imposing, and at first, he found it hard to concentrate on the lessons. He wanted to be outdoors where he could work in the dirt or play in the meadows below the village. Since his friends from the village also went to the class, he felt better. In the winter, the boys would bring in firewood to keep the room warm. In the summer, the room was often too hot. The teacher always held the class no matter what temperature the room was. Stephan worked hard, and he recalls he tried not to fall asleep during the more boring parts of the class like the grammar lessons and the recitations of the teacher from a book in Romanian.

The teacher often spoke about the dangers of the world. He taught the class the history of the Saxon people. He also taught them about the history of Romania and the rest of the world. Stephan recalls learning that the Romanian Army achieved victories over the Germans and Hungarians of the Austrian Empire.[41] It was only because of the strength of the Army of the former Imperial Germany, that Romania was forced to accept a peace treaty in 1916. Had it not done so, Romania would have been destroyed by the combined might of Imperial Germany, the Austro –Hungarian Empire and the Kingdom of Bulgaria.

At least, he recalls, that was how the teacher explained it to a class that had more boys than girls. When the girls were in class, the teacher was more careful about discussing the war because the girls would not be a part of the military. Stephan recalls that it took him a while before it occurred to him that his teacher sometimes used wit and sarcasm. With tongue firmly planted in cheek, he told his students, that after the many victories alongside their allies, France and Britain, Romania came to the table as an equal and gained the territory of Transylvania,[42] but Romania had signed a peace treaty in 1916, before the war ended, and the territory was gained through negotiation at the Paris Peace Talks in 1919. This only made sense to Stephan after he asked his parents and they told him that a delegation to the Talks, lead by Queen Marie of Romania, made this territorial change possible. He also learned that the Saxons voted to unite with Romania. They were loyal Romanian citizens now, and his teacher's history lessons focused on Romania, and its relationship to Transylvania. Stephan knew that Transylvania had been a part of the Kingdom of Hungary during World War One.

Germany now had a new leader, Adolf Hitler, and he united Austria and Germany. The teacher said that Hitler would help the Saxons of Transylvania, but Stephan did not understand why. He knew from all of his lessons that the Saxons never were a part of modern Germany, but he committed this to memory because his teacher emphasized it.

School was interesting to a point, but even at the age of eight, he felt that he had other more important responsibilities.

Stephan spent the winter like any other since he began school. He worked at his lessons in the classroom and at home. He could not produce much enthusiasm for school, but his marks were high enough for his parents to accept, so he never got into any trouble. He recalls that the German language was his favourite subject since he spoke it at home. It came more naturally to him than the Romanian language. He detested some of the other subjects – history and mathematics – with a heretofore-unknown passion. He enjoyed the physical exercises that they did each day before class began more than everything else combined. In the end, this made up for the detestable subjects. The teacher encouraged the children to be healthy, to eat the good food that their parents gave them, and to follow instructions. That was the important idea shaping his life: Follow instructions. He did that even when he was not at school.

By 1938, significant political events began to take place in Europe. At the age of eight, Stephan was still too young to understand all the reasons for the growing concern expressed by the older people around him. Since Stephen was not apt to listen carefully, he only heard a few things. A country called Czechoslovakia had given land to Germany and Hungary. For the first time since the Holy Roman Empire, Austria was united with Germany. Changes were happening in the world, but not to him yet.

He overheard people talk about a war, but war did not mean much to him. He recalls that he equated war with the fort battles the boys carried on in the meadows – no one got hurt, and everyone was friends after their games. He did not understand the difference.

From the way the adults explained things to him, he felt that the war really would not affect anyone in the village too much. Some people might lose some land, and this time it might not be the Germans losing it. This time, the people of Senndorf might even have land returned to them. Stephan reasoned that since the men who led these countries could talk things through, there would never need to be a war. He could learn how to farm and grow up in the hills and meadows of Transylvania, and things would never change. They had not changed much in many years, and Stephan felt that things would never change in the future.

Stephan turned nine in 1939. The winter was not as bad as the year before, or so everyone in his family kept telling him. There was still a lot of snow as far as he could see, and each day he fetched firewood for the schoolroom. That year he noticed something strange: the room looked smaller than it had in the last few years. His clothes also were smaller, and his mother often measured him and sighed. He wondered if it was because he was growing faster, or if things around him were shrinking. He recalls realizing that the one huge room in the school was really two, one for the younger students and one for the older students, but he wondered why one of the rooms looked so large. He decided that he must be growing taller, and that having longer legs might help him win some races during the morning excercises.

The boys of Senndorf loved to run and build forts. He learned how to build a fort quicker and how not to hit his fingers with the hammer. He ran races in the meadows and, he learned a more effective way to run. He would push off with his left foot in a jumping-like motion to propel him faster through the tall grasses. All of this proved to him how much he was growing, and more importantly, that he was improving. They played in the meadows and woods, but they were never out sight of the village itself. They all knew the dangers in the area: There were wolves and bears roaming the forests, and there was fast-moving water nearby. The boys played and enjoyed themselves, and Stephan remembers that they all played safely. The adults instilled this in them; play but be safe. The games the boys played helped them grow strong and hungry, and he loved the food that his mother served at night.

He does not recall a time when he did not eat well, but he thinks he felt hungrier after working in the fresh air. Each evening after dinner, chores, and some studying for the next school day, he joined the other boys out in the gravel streets and in the meadows again to play. He looked forward to the end of school and the planting season.

He was not interested in the vineyards around Senndorf; he found the smell of everything in the vineyard overpowering and full of stinging, angry wasps. The juice was sticky and it stained his hands. He did enjoy seeing the huge oak barrels in the wine storeroom. It was dark and cool in that room, and the men who perfected the wine seemed to be passionate about it. He smiles at me as he recalls how his father helped make wine from the grapes that the family owned and he even had an oak barrel among the others that was passed down to him from his own father. It was the only time Stephan wished someone would teach him how to make wine.

He also wanted to learn how to hunt. He loved accompanying his father when he went hunting for small animals and birds. His father taught him a game so that he could shoot at targets with more accuracy. He was to look first, and then aim the gun, and then take a breath and shoot. As Stephan recalls, he would breathe so loudly that the animal would slow down. Then his father would motion for to him to shoot. At the beginning, the animals he shot were moles and groundhogs that got into the fields and could ruin the crops. He felt proud when he could see them through the green shoots that came out of the earth. It was harder at the end of summer when the golden stalks concealed the little animals – the ones who would eat the corn and wheat. Still, he tried. At the end of summer came two events that he expected: the harvest and the start of a new school year.

He noticed that when his parents and other adults stopped talking in his presence, that she should not ask what they were discussing, but he recalls that he wanted to inquire. Over the next few weeks, the same thing kept happening. He finally asked about it because his curiosity was undeniable. After some hesitation, he asked, and his parents told him that they would explain it to him. He remembers that in the fall of 1939 they told him that Germany was at war with a country called Poland, and that France and Britain were angry about this. They had given Germany time to take their troops out of Poland, and when Germany did not, Britain and France said that they would fight against Germany. This was a satisfactory answer for nine-year-old Stephan, who did not think to ask any more questions.

In June 1940, Stephan heard the news that Germany defeated France. The war was quick, only seven weeks, and Germany had many decisive victories. According to his father, the victory did not cost many lives on the German side. His father explained to him that France sued for peace once Germany proved its military might to the French Army. Stephan was happy that there would be no more fighting and that his father would not have to leave for France. He knew that his father was not obligated to tell him anything, so receiving this information was the highlight of his summer. School would begin and the harvest would come in soon, and he would have new responsibilities.

He was eleven now, and he felt that because he was getting older and could do many of the things that his father could, he asked his parents why they were worrying. His father told him that some new men from outside the country had arrived in Senndorf, but that he did not need to fret. When Stephan enquired if they had come from another village or if they were Hungarians, his father informed him that they came from Germany.[43] He said that they were part of the political party in power there, and they had come to improve the Saxon men in each of the German villages in Hungary. His father said this to him slowly and carefully, letting each word drip with sarcasm. Stephan recalls feeling that this choice of words was unusual, and it made him think back to his teacher's comments. Some of the things he saw began to make sense, and they disconcerted him.

He understood that the men of the village were worried that they might be perceived to be disloyal to Hungary and to Germany. The Saxons of Transylvania were not a part of the Reich or greater Germany; therefore, in Stephan's mind, there was no reason for the men's presence here, and Stephan could see that they had a negative effect on the ordinary traditions of the village. Changes happened after they arrived. Some were small, like learning more about German history and current events in school. Stephan noticed again that these history lessons were not about the Saxons, rather about Germans elsewhere in the world. Other changes, like the new songs that they sang during the evening dances in the village, were more noticeable.

The most significant of the changes was that on Sundays some of the youth would not attend the church service. Instead they gathered outside to sing songs and march. Stephan did not agree with the songs or with not attending church, but he was quick enough to learn to say nothing. Sometimes he received an invitation to join the youth, and he would ask his father who told him he needed to go. His father did not need him to get into trouble, and Stephan would later recall that there was something mesmerizing about those Sundays. Stephan hoped that the summer would be fun and allow him the chance to play, to enjoy time with his friends, and to forget the all-too-dangerous men. He decided that focusing on summer and fun would help him.

His father began to appear more relaxed and joyful, and he told Stephan and his sisters that the German Army was gaining victories against the Russian forces. He told them that he hoped that Russia would surrender and the war would end. Stephan hoped for the same thing, and that the Nazis who made his family so nervous about sharing their own feelings would leave and not return to Senndorf. Stephan believed that the war that began in 1939 caused the Nazis to come to his village and disrupt their lives. Even though he disagreed with the idea of not being in church, he also recalls that he would miss the days away from the church and school out in the bright sunlight marching because sometimes the sermons and lessons were dull.

He studied hard, and he accepted the fact that he would be in school for a few more years; he was eleven after all. In August 1940, Joachim von Ribbentrop and Galeazzo Ciano, the foreign ministers of Germany and Italy, announced a political agreement called the Second Vienna Awards, between Hungary and Romania.[44] His father came to Stephan and his siblings, sat them down, and told them that Senndorf was now a part of Hungary. There would not be a war, simply a change of citizenship. Stephan asked why this happened so quickly, and his father explained that the governments had been in talks for a long time, but it was not important for the children to concern themselves about this.

After much thought, Stephan realized that his parents must have known about it long before they explained it to him, and he chided himself for not listening and for talking too much. At first, he thought that things would change now that they were Hungarian, but then he trusted that his parents would do what was best for their children. He might not enjoy the new rules or new taxes, but he would not complain. He worried less when nothing in the church or school changed from the traditions that he grew up in. The teacher did say something new was going to happen the next year. He did not tell the class what it would be, but Stephan did not worry.

Stephan recalls that he very much welcomed the change at school. Instead of learning Romanian language and history, as they had done every year before, the class would now learn about Hungary. The teacher informed the class that since the villagers of Senndorf were now loyal Hungarian citizens and Hungary was a loyal supporter of Germany, the students would learn Hungarian along with the German language. Stephan recalls that he wondered why the teacher insisted that the children be loyal citizens. Northern Transylvania had only recently joined the country of Hungary in November, after a 21 year absence, so why should there need to be this much loyalty from the young children? He dismissed this notion to the back of his mind; it was not important to him.

In 1941, Stephan felt that his schoolwork was harder to learn. He dutifully studied his Hungarian lessons. He found it to be more enjoyable than learning Romanian, but it was still less interesting than the physical exercises in the morning. Later, he would appreciate that each part of his schooling served him well at some point in his life: The physical education helped him with his strength, and the languages allowed him to adapt to his life outside of the village. He worked hard at his lessons because his parents had impressed upon him the value of hard work and excellence in everything that he did.

The teacher spent a lot of time talking about the values that the powerful German people had in their great history. Stephan saw that these lessons were really about the Germans from Germany and had nothing to do with Transylvania. It was not about the German defeats that everyone knew about, but how their opponents undermined the Germans and engineered those defeats. This was especially true of the last War, which ended in 1918. He recalled the teacher's look of distaste when he talked about it, and he recalls the fear that his teacher seemed to have. The teacher mentioned little about the German Empire, founded in 1871, except for the politicians, specifically Otto von Bismarck. The teacher did not teach them about the monarchies, and he never spoke of German kings or emperors in recent history.[45] Stephan recalls that he did not pay much attention to that fact until his father pointed out that the emperors held most of the power in both Germany and imperial Austria until 1918.

School was Stephan's most important responsibility, but since he was a young boy, he had some freedoms from work. Saturdays meant he could go into the forest and cut wood with the other boys, and often his father came along to use the axe or a saw to bring down the larger trees. He enjoyed seeing the trees fall, and he recalls that his father always warned him to pay attention to where the tree might land. Sometimes Stephan and his father would cut the wood into smaller pieces for the family fireplace, or they would make planks and other pieces of wood that the village might need. They used the planks for making chairs, tables, and beds for the families of Senndorf.

Stephan did not enjoy woodworking that much, but he knew that helping where he could in Senndorf was all a part of being in a community. The village offered opportunities to help in every aspect of life. There was much work to do and very few people to do it. Each family had their own piece of land that they were responsible for, but the men of the village would help their neighbours when they needed it. Sometimes, though, help meant not telling the young boys about current world affairs.

By the end of October of 1940, Stephan recalls that it had already snowed and it was colder than normal; he remembers trying to do everything he could to keep warm[46]. It was a race against time to store the harvested crops properly before the frost ruined them and to bring the livestock in before any were injured or died from exposure. The animals were very valuable and no farmer wanted any of them to die because of his own negligence. His father made sure that the oxen and horses were protected from the gusts of wind, and that they had enough food should no one be able to get to the animals' shelter in a blizzard. They herded the pigs and sheep into another stall to keep them warm as well. Even though some would be slaughtered for food, they still needed attention. They could also sell pigs and sheep at the market in Bistritz for money to buy supplies and treats. He knew that although the taxes were now lower, they still amounted to a lot of money. There were times when a family could not pay the taxes, and the officials would take away the men's good clothes until they paid. Sometimes these families would come to church in the best clothes they could find, their everyday clothes. Stephan never looked down on them because he knew that everyone tried as hard as they could, and each person could only do so much. He overheard comments from his father, who often had trouble paying taxes as well, but he also overheard things about the war.

By the end of October 1941, the war was going badly for Germany in Russia, but there were some victories and many promises that the German Army would crush the Russians soon. The men from Germany proclaimed it loudly to the villagers of Senndorf. Some of the village men hoped that this was true, but others who still had memories of the First World War, did not. Stephan overheard those men talk about Russia being this war's America,[47] an invincible war machine, unleashed and unstoppable, that would crush the very life out the German Army. From what he had learned in his history class, he understood what they meant, but he felt that it was premature to think that way; after all, there had been some victories, and not many men had left for the front. When he mentioned this to his father, his father commented with one word: "Yet." Stephan understood that the war was not over and they would see what would happen in the next year.

Stephan enjoyed their hunting trips and spending time with his father, and he found that his aim was better than the year before. His father told him that with practice, he would be able to shoot larger animals for food. He remembers that his father was stern about when and how he should use the guns. They were not used for anything but shooting game, and Stephan repeated this to his father before and after each use: "Only for game, never on people." The summer passed by quickly, and life in Senndorf was uneventful. Some world events stood out in his mind, though, and the month of June was one like no other. There was more fighting, and hundreds of unfolding battles.

The boys built enormous wooden forts and pretended to be opposing armies. Of course, Stephan recalls that in their games, the German Army always won after nearly being defeated. The older men smiled wanly at their creative antics and let them play. Stephan knows now that it was because they wanted the boys to have the chance to dream and understand that they could just be boys. However, for all their seemingly wondrous turnaround victories, the defeats of the real German Army grew, and Stephan still hoped for one large quick victory against the communist foe. He recalls that it was the naïve hope of a young boy.

At age of fourteen, his confirmation later in the year and his impending transition to manhood excited him because he believed it meant people would begin to listen to him more and value his opinions. It also meant the end of his formal schooling. He felt his time could be better spent working alongside his father and mother in the fields. He knew that one day he would inherit this land, and he would be the man of the household. He would eventually serve in the army and get married. He wanted to live his life as a farmer; that was the only thing he knew for sure. His focus for this upcoming harvest was to help with bringing in the crops faster. He enjoyed the hard work, and he decided that he would help in any way that he could, even though he was young. The days were getting shorter, and in the mountains of Transylvania, the sun seemed to set faster.

He wanted to be doing more things that did not involve school. He still enjoyed the physical activities that the class did each morning, and found that the other subjects still did not interest him as much. Later he would recall that all of his lessons did serve him well at different points in his life, but at the time, he did not appreciate it that much. He learned more German language and history, and the history lessons particularly stood out in his mind. The teacher spent a lot of time talking about the values and traditions of the mighty German people. Stephan saw again that this history was really about the Germans from Germany and had nothing to do with Transylvania or the Saxons. He learned the Hungarian language and helped with the chores such as collecting firewood and cleaning the schoolroom. There was always work to be done. His father needed his help more that year, too, and Stephan looked forward to that.

The days passed quickly. He asked his father how he used to figure out the time of the day in the years before there were clocks or other time-keeping devices in Senndorf. His father told him that in the house, they used to use candles that burned for an hour each, and outside the sundial guided them. He also told Stephan to look hard at nature. Stephan saw that the leaves were changing and falling and that the temperature was cooling. He was pleased when his father agreed with his observations. He knew it was time to harvest when he saw the wheat turned a golden colour and the corn ripened, and his father showed him how to see if the corn was ready to harvest. He peeked at the ears of corn each day to see the colour inside and he would tell his father that he thought it was ready. His father kept telling him that it was not. One day though, his father agreed, and Stephan was pleased and helped with harvesting the corn.

Stephan still did not enjoy school. This school year began the same way as the one before, and the teacher expected each student to perform better than he or she had done last year. Stephan did enjoy the school for the time he could spend with his friends. Even though he did not enjoy the lessons, he still worked hard to get good grades – or at least grades that were acceptable to his parents. He recalls that in some subjects, a passing grade was sufficient and Current Events was one of these. The teacher did not seem to enjoy the subject either, and gave the impression that he wanted the class to learn other things. Otherwise, the school year continued on following the routine set long ago. Stephan gleefully looked forward to Christmas and the time he would be able to spend with his family.

He enjoyed that Christmas. His mother made good food, and he received some unexpected toys; a duck whistle and a miniature wooden shotgun. All of the toys were simple but made especially for each child. He wanted the coming year to be better than the last one and free from the worry about events happening in Russia.

Stephan recalls men leaving and women worrying about their husbands at the front. Many of the women who seemed so young grew old before his eyes; the stress of each day and the unknown fates of husbands, sons, and brothers hung heavily on them. His father was older, so he did not need to go. Stephan's strongest memory is of the haggard look his father had over the news that one division or another in Russia suffered massive casualties. Many famous army divisions were decimated, and he recalls that, to his father's horror, many of these divisions had friends of his father in them. Their deaths were almost certain. When his father received bad news, he would come home, sit by the fire, and not talk. Although the house was warm and cheery most of the time, Stephan felt a gloom whenever his father returned. As much as he wanted to talk with his father, he realized that it was the war in Russia and the fear of fighting that made his father worry. Stephan did not want to fight either, not for Germany at least, but he thought about how long this war was running. He decided he would only fight if necessary.

The last war, the Great War, was four years long, and Germany only began to suffer major losses in the final year. Stephan reasoned that since this war was now in its fifth year, it might be three more years before it ended. He mentioned this to his father, who smiled and said perhaps not, because the war was already going badly for the German Army. Stephan recalls that he never heard that the war was going badly for the Germans, though. He did not ask how his father knew this, and he later realized that his father must have deduced it from the radio announcements. He began paying attention to what people said when they talked about the war. Stephan noticed that the radio announcer always talked about small victories, a kilometre here or there. There was no word of the promised crushing defeat of the Russians. The Russians were winning some impressive victories, and the formerly invincible German

Army was in disarray. The official announcements gave some vague numbers, but most people knew the truth despite what official notices and radio broadcasts reported. Stephan also noted that the distance between the battles and his home was decreasing. He had no desire to ask further. The visiting Nazis made certain of this.

In some ways, the war still seemed to be a grand adventure; he was young and at the moment, the army did not need his services. At 14, he was not close to the age for becoming a soldier. He never mentioned this to his parents, for they valued life above everything else, and had he told them, he knows it would have horrified and saddened them – as if they failed in some way in instilling that value in him. He found himself wanting to fight, not for Germany, but for his family, his village and his home. His sisters could not fight, but he could. He was good with a gun – he had been using one for years now to hunt, and perhaps that would allow him to fight better. He was tall and well built, and he was stronger than most of the other boys his age. He could do more to help. How he could do that he was not yet certain, but somehow he would find a way.

The news about the war grew steadily worse. He could feel the tension in the village growing with each kilometre that the Russian Army marched closer to Senndorf. He overheard people talking about scorched earth, and to his dismay, he learned the Russian military was deliberately burning anything it its path. This was a dangerous time. He heard new sounds that did not seem to be a part of the natural landscape. It seemed like there were hundreds of thousands of airplanes overhead now; some were heading eastward and some, more ominously, were heading westward. At the end of the summer of 1944, the announcement came over the radio ordering all the Saxons of Northern Transylvania to evacuate. They were to depart by no later than the middle of September.

The Russians were on the move, and they were going to destroy everything and everyone. If any of the Saxons stayed behind, they would most certainly die. There were rumours about Russian labour camps. The villagers feared leaving but they knew that they must, it was an order from Arthur Phelps, the Saxon Army commander in northern Transylvania.

Stephan recalls that at that point, too, he did not fear the bullets, and he did not seem to worry about being injured or dying. The Russian soldiers were doing their job. In a way, he envied them; they could take action. He remained in the village helping the old men and young boys do work for the families whose men who were away – many of them at the Russian front or in Yugoslavia. He did not enjoy parts of the work, like pulling the oxen and saddling the remaining horses, or making repairs to homes and the church. He wanted to be anywhere but working on the boring chores, but he needed to keep himself busy and make some money for his family. He knew that the evacuation was his chance to survive, but in some small way, he felt like he would be running away, not simply from his home, but from his beloved way of life. His heart demanded action, but his mind told him that it would result in a dishonourable death.

They finished the harvest and some other work around the house and farm, and they packed some basic food baskets. Stephan and his father walked beside the wagon that his mother and sisters rode in. The evacuation was slow. The road was covered with debris from the bombed-out train tracks beside it, and the roaring of planes overhead and bombs falling from them caused the horses to buck and panic. Pilots sometimes saw the wagon trains and fired at them. The noise sent everyone running from the road to hide wherever they could, but some people were killed by the bombs. Stephan recalls he often needed to calm the horses before he could take cover.

He received his opportunity to fight sooner than he thought he would.[48] Stephan did not so much volunteer for the army, as much as army personnel selected him. To his delight, he found the training simpler than anticipated. The German Army, under the command of the Nazi Party, needed as many men as they could find. Their age did not matter; the only requirement was that the men or boys could shoot. If not, Stephan recalls that they received some basic training. He had already gained experience with a rifle while spending time with his father.

He recalls the military encampment was a group of large tents teeming with boys of all ages; he found out later that some of them were as young as 12 years old. The training consisted of waking up early and shooting at targets for hour after hour. His drill sergeant was pleased with his skill. Stephan recalls that, had the war not ended when it did, he might have become a sniper because his aim was so accurate.

The monotony of doing the same training each day began to irritate him, and he voiced his disapproval of it. He wanted action, not more practice. His commanders told him no and reprimanded him. He should wait and be silent. He remained irritated and silent, but he believed that he could have helped bring victory for the Germans. He recalls that he realized many months later, that he could not have won the war alone, but in that moment he longed to be heroic and full of action. He never wanted to be defeated. He recalls that death did not seem as bad as some men reported it to be. Even though he did not want the war to continue, he wished for the opportunity to fight.

Stephan recalls that the end of the war was not as simple or as quick as many people describe it. Thousands of people were separated from their families, and he was one those people. He was young and unarmed, and he was not required to go into a prisoner of war camp because he had not fought in the war as some had. He knew that if he was captured, he would be sent to one of the Russian labour camps. He knew how fortunate he was that he did not go to Russia. The possibility of his death was high. He might have survived, but not as a whole man.

In 1944, he was still far away from his parents and sisters who had continued their journey to the border of Germany. He fretted that they might have returned to Transylvania without his knowledge. To his relief, he learned from army officers that his family was still alive and living near the Austrian-German border. He felt that there was always good news and bad news. He heard that the Saxons had lost everything in the war, and if they returned to their villages, they no longer owned their house and land. He assumed for a while that it meant the houses were destroyed. They were not, but now the Romanians of the village owned and occupied them.

Much of the rail line to Germany was destroyed by bombs, so he set out on foot. He worried that he might encounter men from either the Russian or the American Armies. From the stories he heard, either army's soldiers would kill a stranger on sight. While he assumed this was true of the Russians, he was not as certain about the Americans. He remembered that many of the Saxons had gone to work in America, and they had returned with glowing stories of the life they led. It seemed that America had treated them well, and they did not have to pay as much tax. He decided that he would prefer to face a squad of armed Americans rather than Russians, and they might show him mercy.

His greatest fear was that he might loose his way through the forest and find himself in lands far from his family, alone. Stephan stayed positive and remembered that he was not helpless. His parents taught him a great deal about how to survive. Bearing this thought in his mind, he set out toward the northwest. The trip was monotonous, but at least he never saw any soldiers.

What he did see is etched in his memory. There was a constant flow of refugees towards Germany, and Stephan recalls the hoards of people, terrorized and fearful. Many of them had never lived within the borders of Germany, or even within the former borders of Imperial Germany. These people looked exhausted and starved in many cases, and they would run at the sight of anyone they did not know. Stephan recalls that the women seemed especially fearful. At the time, he did not understand that the dangers of being in a country East of Transylvania meant that looting and raping and death abounded. Many people he met told him what the Russian Army had done to them, and he recalls his anger and horror when he learned about these atrocities. Inwardly, his rage boiled, and he longed to find a gun and kill the Russian soldiers doing these things.

It shamed him when he learned about the atrocities the Nazis committed, and he felt guilty about enjoying the marches when he was younger. His mind went to the horrible treatment of injured soldiers, often killed by their own government. Innocent civilians' lives lost simply because they were in some way physically or mentally disabled, or they followed a different religion.[49] He remains convinced, however, that the marches in and of themselves were fun and enjoyable. In this way, he valued the positive and not the negative. He knew that for the Germans who lived within the borders of Germany during the war, their conscience – or guilt – was far more painful than his own was. At least he did not live anywhere near where these horrid things had happened. He decided that he would not think about them anymore, and he continued toward his ultimate destination, his family.

After many weeks of wandering and fretting, he found them. Although they were safe in a small community in Germany where many of the Transylvanian Saxons now resided, it felt as if they moved the entire Saxon nation to this small city on a hill. It was hot and overcrowded. Few people found work beyond that of a day labourer, and Stephan took work whenever and wherever he could. He wanted something more, though, and he decided that along with his parents and sisters, he would emigrate across the ocean. Many Saxons had already made the decision to go to Canada, and so that was the logical choice. Moving there meant that he would need to learn a new language; however, he realized that this would not be too great a challenge to meet since he had already learned some new languages in his school days.

Canada proved to be an adventure well suited to his personality. There were many Saxons in their new town, and many of them kept traditions from Transylvania. He was encouraged by the many dances and picnics that took place here, and he met his future wife at one of these events in 1952. She was young, the youngest daughter of one of the prominent men who pushed to keep the traditions of the Saxons alive. Matilde was an elegant, statuesque young woman, and her sense of humour matched his own. To Stephan's delight, they shared much in common; the only difference was that she was soft-spoken and rarely argued. Later, though, he enjoyed encouraging her to speak up about her ideas and opinions.

They married with many people in attendance, and it was one of the few times he wore a tuxedo. He recalls that he detested it, since he thought it made him look daft, but Matilde wanted it that way. Soon after the wedding, their first child, a son, arrived. Stephan did not name his son after himself, though, which was a break with tradition. He knew that it would only cause confusion in their ever-expanding family; his parents and in-laws now counted close to 10 grandchildren between them. He was overjoyed that he had a son and could pass on the traditions and life lessons that he had once learned.

They lived with her family for a time after they were married. A few years later, they bought a nice house and raised their family. Stephan worked hard but he was always careful to find time to go hunting, and he enjoyed that pastime. When he retired, he found it hard not to be working, so he went into business for himself, cleaning and doing work in the yards in the city.

"Afterwards," Stephan comments, "things went along efficiently." He worked and he hunted. He has a good life. He glances towards his wife, and she shrugs her shoulders. "I didn't miss anything," he protests. "I even mentioned the yahoos, children."

"You forgot two," is her counterargument.

"I did not!" He counts his fingers. "Okay, there were two more, and I still hunted, and raised my two boys and daughter."

I ask, "Daughter?"

"Well, yes, she's a daughter, not a girl. You cannot do things with a daughter that you can with boys. Besides," he intones, "she didn't like the hunting dogs." His wife makes a mild guffaw.

To Be More Than History

He is one of the few men in the village who learned how to ride a bicycle. He used it transport goods for his family. Now he can put this skill to another use: Delivering messages between the fighting units at war with the Russian Army. There is so much death. He was young and foolish he knows now, but he had a duty and that was to ride this bicycle to the next unit with information. Fewer men might die this way.

He doesn't know it yet, but the field he drives across is mined and at any moment, he might wheel over one, and he might die or lose a leg. The war is not going well, and he feels certain he will die. He pedals forward...

Andreas starts by telling me to speak up because he is getting old. Some days he might be right, but on other days, he acts young, and I forget, and then he asks me again. His voice is full of wisdom gained from both experience and learning. He always has a smile on his face, and is willing to talk about his lost life; not what might have been but what was. It is always more important to know what was, and to Andreas that is the vital piece to life.

He also enjoys reading, and when his wife quietly reminds him that he does not need to read all that much, he retorts that how else is he supposed to learn? He is getting older, and he feels obligated to share the history of his people to others. He seems so intent on telling the big-picture story that I almost hesitate to ask him anything specific about his life. He will tell me about his own experiences, he tells me with a mild chortle, provided that he can share his knowledge of the traditions of the Saxons with me in return.

Andreas was born in Burghalle, a small farming village to the south of the major city Bistritz. In 1926, there was no maternity ward or hospital nearby, and families always worried that a birth would not be easy. This one was. After all seemed well, Andreas was baptized in the Burghalle Lutheran Church.

Andreas enjoyed his childhood, and he recalls the festivities held during the year the most. All the Saxons in Burghalle attended. The brass band always played music. Andreas longed to be able to learn how to play a musical instrument so he could play in the group once he grew older. He loved the music that the band played, and he thought the woodwind instruments, especially the clarinet, added a beautifying effect. For him, the highlight of the night was the singing, and he loved that everyone knew the songs the group sang. People seemed happy during these evenings. The hard work that the men did in the fields each day seemed to be justified when they could all come together and enjoy an evening of singing and laughter. The only unpleasant part of each dance was when his mother sent him home early because she feared that her son would get too excited and be unable to fall asleep. At the age of seven, he had to get up early the next morning for school.

School was always an important focus in his life, even when tragedy struck. Andreas recalls that he was seven years old when he started, and that his father died later that same year after a long illness. For him, these two events are interlinked and he will often mention one at the same time as the other. The times when classes began and ended are etched in his memory. He rose early in the morning to complete his chores and then class began.

Andreas recalls his father fondly but faintly. He knows that his father loved him and his siblings. He remembers his father's funeral unfolded according to Saxon tradition: his father wore the white shirt that he wore on his wedding day, everyone from the village attended the funeral service, and the band played music in the church and at the cemetery. Andreas does not know exactly what illness caused his father's death, but he wonders if a combination of age and hard work contributed to it. Andreas was nearly sixteen years younger than his two sisters, and he was born later in his father's life.

Whatever the reason was, his mother and sisters all began to do work that was normally reserved for men. Andreas was still a child, though, and there were two important things that he needed to worry about: school and caring for the fields. Even with these responsibilities, there was always time for play and for nurturing passions, one of which was learning about history.

Over the years, Andreas discovered that he learned best from practical examples. It was important to him to know why and how to preserve the history and traditions of the Saxons in Burghalle for his children and grandchildren. He remembers that his teacher might not have enjoyed the mandatory languages lessons that he taught the students, but he became animated when he spoke about the traditions of the Saxons. The lessons about history and tradition helped Andreas and gave him a sense of stability in his life, provided people continued these traditions. By the age of twelve, he saw changes in the village that affected his family.

In 1938, he remembers that the men of Burghalle were excited about Austria and Germany merging into one larger country[50]. When Andreas asked why they did this, the answer was so that Germany would become great again. He could see that the men in the village hoped that this would help them to gain more freedoms in Romania. After all, there were taxes to pay, and this was often a challenge for many of the farmers. He knew from his lessons that the Saxons and Hungarians lost land to the Romanians after the First World War. However, he could not understand why people were excited about the merger because it happened so far away.

In the fall of 1939, the harvest started as normal, but news from outside of the village dominated conversations. Andreas remembers he overheard the men talking about a country called Poland and so he looked it up on the map in the schoolroom. He remembers that it seemed so far away to him, and he wondered why anyone here should worry about it. But many people in Burghalle worried, and he overheard them talk about "France" and "Britain"; then "war" and "Germany"[51]. He began to understand, without asking, that the world might once again be at war. In some ways, Andreas thought it would be an adventure, and perhaps when it was over Germany would be stronger and the Saxon people would find themselves better off. He was not sure if this was the best way to go about being better, but he hoped that in the end, the world would not fight again for four years – as it had during World War I.

Andreas entered his final year of school in the spring of 1939 and he looked forward to new responsibilities in his village. Burghalle was small but he loved its traditions. He still looked forward to running the family farm on his own one day. Before he could take on that responsibility, he needed to be confirmed in the church, and so he studied his lessons in both school and church with an intensity that he did not previously know that he had. He remembers that he did a lot of work between playing and studying. Andreas remembers that under normal circumstances, his cousins and uncles would help when they could once they had completed their own work in their part of the hills. The crops were delayed because of a later than normal snow and frost. He worried that because everyone was so busy with their own planting he would not have as much help this year. He and his mother worked together to get all the seed into the ground that they could. Andreas accepted the help that he received, and he knew that in a few years he would need to work the land on his own with the help of his mother and sister.

Once the planting season ended, he had more time to himself to be just what he was: a young boy playing with his friends.

He knew that he only had one more year before his time would not be his own but would be structured according to the responsibilities of adulthood. He enjoyed running races and playing games in wooden forts that he and his friends constructed with increasing skill. He still had small responsibilities around the farm, like weeding and keeping the small animals out of the fields, but in comparison to planting or harvesting, these were simple. The outdoors and the fresh air did him good, he remembers, and he grew stronger and taller that year. He began to help in the village's vineyards making sure that the grapes grew without disease and that the vines stayed on the stakes and arches that the men of Burghalle built. When it rained, Andreas and his friends enjoyed the chance to be indoors, and they played cards and board games to occupy their time. Soon the summer ended and the harvest would come. For Andreas this year's harvest was more memorable than some others. Two events linked together – one before and one after the harvest – remained in his memory long afterwards.

In June 1940, as the men began to talk about what crops to harvest first (though there really was no debate and more of an agreement) the radio announced the defeat of France. He was excited since he felt that with this victory, the Saxons would have new rights and prestige; the people of Burghalle were Germans after all. Andreas did not resent the fact that the Saxons lost land, but he was bitter that they had to pay high taxes. He remembered that, to him, Germany becoming powerful meant that the Saxons could be better off. When the harvest started in earnest, Andreas helped his mother cut and collect the hay, and then the corn, and finally all the vegetables from the hills. Once this was completed, he helped cut down the hemp so that they could use it for making clothes. His uncles asked him to help with cutting the grapes in the vineyards. He did not like doing this much because the grapes often broke and the juice would leave stains and marks on his shirt. He could never understand how his mother could clean his shirts so perfectly.

In August of 1940, excitement in the village grew when Hungary gained the territory of Northern Transylvania from Romania as part of the Second Vienna Award. Andreas hoped that Hungary might regain the rest of Transylvania through more arbitration and there might not be the war that he heard many men discussing. He knew that he needed to listen and learn, but because he was not yet confirmed, he did not feel that anyone valued his opinions. Across Transylvania, many parents did their best to protect their young children from the worst news, but they were also careful to show them that life did not bring good things all the time.

Even though many responsibilities of the farm were placed on Andreas's young shoulders, he still received help from his uncles and cousins. He went to school and to church. In the evenings after all his chores and schoolwork were complete, he loved to go to the dances where he could sing and enjoy himself. Advent and Lent were the only two times during the year that there were no dances held in the village. Andreas recalls that this was because both seasons were an important time for reflection in the church. In the winter, the dances provided a welcome break from the cold outdoors and the miles of pristine snow. The hall in Burghalle was decorated with ribbons and embroidered white blankets that the women of the village made themselves.

The band would play until well past midnight, by which time Andreas needed to leave so that he was ready to start classes. The dances did not happen each day and often not each week, but everyone would have plenty of fun. Attending these events and learning the songs and dances meant Andreas could carry on traditions of his village and of the Saxon people, and it gave him a sense of pride to know that he might eventually pass them on to the next generation.

Since the end of August 1940, and the radio in the Burghalle hall announced that Northern Transylvania was no longer a part of Romania, and the villagers were Hungarian citizens there was much debate between the men.

Andreas was excited about the prospect of being Hungarian. He heard many stories about how the people fared better in Transylvania when Hungary was a part of the Austro-Hungarian Empire, than now under Romanian rule. He knew how much tax men had to pay and often they would not have enough left over to feed their families properly. He hoped that once he was confirmed next year, the taxes would be lower and that food would be more plentiful. He dreamed of the days when he would be able to provide more for his future children. He also knew that not everything that was in the past was good, but he wondered if perhaps life might improve under the rule of the Hungarians. He knew that he would find out over the course of the coming years.

For Andreas, 1941 was his year of destiny. He turned fifteen, and he was confirmed in the Burghalle church in front of his family on Palm Sunday.

As much as he enjoyed the evenings that he spent singing and dancing, the outdoors proved more alluring. The snow on the hills was melting and it filled the creek in the village with rushing water. Andreas remembers how careful everyone needed to be; otherwise someone could fall in and drown. No one did, but parents constantly reminded the boys and girls not to go near the water for a while until all the snow had melted. The boys received more warnings since the parents felt that they would get into more trouble and misadventures than the girls would, but the girls often joined in until they were confirmed.

The planting and confirmation season, as Andreas thought of it, was fast approaching and he wanted to complete the planting on time or sooner than was expected of him. He worked late into the evenings, helping his mother by carrying large burlap sacks, used for grain and corn storage, to the open shed where they would treat them with lye to protect them from various fungus and moulds. He moved the bags of corn so that he could access them faster when he needed them. They planted some of it in the fields and used some for animal feed, so he needed to know which bag was for which purpose. He made sure the yokes for the oxen stayed dry and no mould grew on them. His mother told him that he did not have to do all these chores right away, but Andreas remembers how strongly he felt that he needed to do the work before any of the other men in his family told him it was time to do it. He wanted to show the men of Burghalle that he could run the plough and plant the fields himself because he would soon be the man of the house. His mother helped him as best she could but she seemed to understand that he needed to show his worth.

With the planting season also came confirmation, and for Andreas, confirmation was more memorable than the planting season this year. It officially marked his transition from boy to man in the eyes of the villagers. Although, he comments that if his father had lived, this would be more accurate but he was already doing a man's duty in the fields long before this point.

The teenage men of Burghalle had a group that all the newly-confirmed boys were invited to join. Andreas does not recall that anyone ever declined this invitation, and each youth was happy to be a part of this group[52]. It gave the young men the chance for fun and fellowship when they had time away from working in the fields. Now he was able to join in the dances and the games that they had, and to have fun with his friends, even when everyone was so busy.

Andreas could not think of anything better than to spend an evening with his friends. He noticed that some of the men were quieter and more thoughtful than before, though. He had heard about the men who came to the village from Germany, but he does not recall any of them coming to speak with him or anyone else. It is possible that, because he was so young and he did not have a father, they believed he would not cause trouble. He concentrated on the work he needed to do in the hills and at home.

He tried to find time to learn anything he could about how to run his family farm well, and he found that the taxes he had to pay were less than before. Other than the worry over paying taxes (as the man of the house he was now responsible for doing this) the summer of 1941 unfolded as any other. Then the radio announced that Germany and Russia were now at war. He cannot remember precisely when he heard it, but the next announcement told them that Hungary, as an ally of Germany, was at war with Russia, too.

Andreas, like many of the younger men, felt that Germany would win a great victory against the communist foes. He was excited since this meant that perhaps Germany, and by extension the Saxons, would gain more freedoms[53]. Andreas felt that his people lost too much too quickly at the end of the last war, after Transylvania became a part of Romania. Andreas recalls that some people were worried about leaving for war, but during the summer months, he heard only about victories over the radio and he was glad. He recalls that, for many men, these victories meant that history might not repeat itself.

Andreas was too young to remember the First World War, and his mother would not say anything about it. He hoped that the constant victory announcements might mean the war would end quickly[54]. Germany held much of Europe and, if Russia surrendered, he thought that perhaps there would be more land for the Saxons in Transylvania. He heard the stories that the older men told about the land that the Romanian government took away from them after the end of The First World War. There were times when he imagined having more land where he could farm and hire people to help him. He hoped for the best, though, and began to prepare for the harvest.

He recalls that the men had very strict ideas about who did what within the village. Women were not expected to do hard farm work, but they helped with lighter duties in the fields and caring for the vineyards, vegetable gardens and family homes.

He remembers realizing that those tasks really were not light work, but that is how the men viewed life in Burghalle.

The start of the winter season began with dances and singing, and there was time to relax now that the farm work was complete. The village hall filled with young and happy people, but their conversations and discussions later in the evenings were tinted with worry about the men who might leave. The announcements on the radio began to tell of defeats of the German army in Russia, and Andreas worried that this might mean that they would have to send more horses and men from Burghalle to help. Many of the older men, the ones who would need to go to the front, worried that if defeats continued there would be more deaths and that the danger would come close to Burghalle.

The last war had not affected the Saxons in as many ways. The men dutifully went away to the fighting front where many of them died or were injured, but Andreas remembers that most people around him felt that, however that war ended, the village and people of Burghalle stayed safe from harm. He prayed in church that the men who went away would remain safe and that God would protect his family and the village. He hoped that the season would end in good news, and it was only two months until the end of the year.

The winter proved cold. Andreas could not recall a winter much colder and longer than this one. He remembers that as 1941 became 1942 the blanket of snow that covered most of the landscape arrived early and stayed late. He decided that he was still young, though, and there might be colder winters. His mother knitted woollen socks and worked with the other village women to make clothes from the hemp that they collected from the low-lying fields close to the river. He chopped wood near his house to keep the stove going for longer periods. At night, he often woke up to place more wood on the fire. He was thankful for the warm blankets on his bed. His family's house was solid, and the wind did not blow through it, so the only time when he got cold was when he walked to the hall or the church. Once inside, the people and their chatter and the strong buildings kept him warm. As the end of this year approached quickly, Andreas began to think about the things he needed to do to get a better crop in the coming one. He believed that the life he knew would go on as before, and the war would not touch him directly; it was too far away and he was still young enough not to fear going to fight in Russia.

Andreas spent as much time as he could watching people and learning the village's traditions. Although, at the time, he did not suspect that his ability for the written word would be much use. He would later write two books about the history of the Saxon people and his village Burghalle. He was a farmer and that was the most important thing in his life. After Christmas, there were dances in the Burghalle hall. He enjoyed them and participated as best he could. He does not remember how well he danced or with whom, but he is certain that these were still the highlights of his life. In spite of the fun, he also knew that some responsibilities would never end, and soon he would need to begin planting and caring for the fields so that the seeds would grow.

The only time when it was hard for him to plough or harrow was when the rain was falling hard, but he made every effort to do the work. He accepted that if he did not finish preparing the field, then the planting and harvest would happen too late.

He did not have to worry much. Planting went well and his mother was pleased with all his effort. He remembers that the food he ate each day was excellent, and he admits that it was most likely even better because he was hungry after the long day of work. He told this to his mother who laughed and replied that his father had often said the same thing. Andreas was pleased that there were ways he was similar to his father. With the planting complete, the summer's arrival meant that he could relax somewhat, and he enjoyed caring for the plants during the day and going to the dances at night. He was also able to take time and deepen his understanding of the culture in which he grew up.

He remembers that he felt carefree, but he sensed also a tension in the village that he did not like. The older men talked of Russia and of war. Some men even left for areas outside the country. Some of the men left because they reached the age when Hungary required them to serve in the army. The worries of the older men did not affect Andreas as much as some of the other boys, but he was not oblivious to the changes in the men. He was more concerned that Burghalle was losing horses to the war effort than he was about the news that the losses by the German forces in Russia were mounting.

The mechanized divisions were losing, and he overheard some men commenting that the army was using horses and wagons again. Andreas dismissed this as gossip because he heard over the radio that the German army was gaining ground, especially in Southern Russia. He was not sure what to believe, but he hoped that these reported losses were not the foreshadowing of a total defeat because after the last war, the village lost land to the Romanians. When he mentioned this, some of the men pointed out to him that the Romanians were allies with Hungary and would likely protect Hungary if the Russian army advanced. He decided that it was best to worry about the harvest and not about a far away war that did not affect him personally.

Andreas felt that this year's abundant harvest was a good omen for everyone; the work was harder since there were fewer horses but everyone helped each other to get the work done. He loaded the wagon full of wheat to take to the mill, and then he brought home the flour. He did this several times over the course of the harvest. He helped with taking down the vines and putting them under burlap bags to protect them from the snow and cold of the mountains. To his dismay, someone told him that this might be a final harvest for him in Transylvania – a possibility that he did not like to consider.

He tried to ignore the gossip from the women who lived in the village. He did not have anything against them, but he didn't find it interesting; they usually talked about who was courting whom and who was going to get married or have a child. These days, though, he noticed that the women spoke of one thing: the war and he could see that they looked at him differently. Many of the men his age had left for the front, and he was still home. He began to consider leaving as well and doing his duty for the Hungarian army.

He knew that by 1943, he would be seventeen and therefore old enough to serve in the Hungarian Army. He wondered if he should not do more for his country than stay in the village caring for the farm and working the land that his friends and family had left when they joined the army. He waited and wondered.

In September 1944, before he had time to think about the matter further, another announcement came over the radio: the Saxons must leave their homes and head into Austria[55]; the war was closing in on them and they would be killed or worse, if the Russians caught them. Andreas could not believe his ears, and he recalls that he purposefully avoided looking at the other men for fear of seeing the looks of despair and anger on their faces. Andreas was grief-stricken when he finally understood that he might need to leave home in what he felt was such a dishonourable fashion, but he was excited and wanted to help in any way he could; it was an adventure, after all.

The families packed their belongings quickly. His main responsibilities were to load the wagon as efficiently as possible. There was no time to waste on trivial items; food and clothes were all they needed. Each day brought the roaring of planes overhead and the booming sounds of artillery exchanges. The danger of remaining in Burghalle rapidly increased. Andreas recalls that it only took three days to prepare before they were ready. The long line of haggard villagers and exhausted men helping with the wagons began to move. The journey was slow, too slow to Andreas, and he felt that it was made even slower by the oxen. The thought kept running through his head that they needed to go faster to escape, but the oxen would not move any faster. He envied his mother who remained perfectly calm through the entire seven-week-long journey.

Andreas was not a soldier but he assumed a responsibility to protect and serve the Saxons in Austria. Messages needed to go between the dispersed groups from Transylvania. They needed to coordinate between each other and those who remained in Transylvania. The men at the front also needed to be informed of the progress of the millions being evacuated. Andreas could ride a bicycle. He had learned how to do this a number of years ago, so he volunteered. He could barely contain his enthusiasm for helping with this vital service in the war.

The morning he received his first assignment, he needed to bike across many miles of mine-strewed fields, but he did not find out right away about the mines. They told him to avoid the roads where he would be targeted; fields were safer. He had nightmares for weeks after he found out about the danger. He had nightmares about the explosions and his broken bleeding body lying in the sun only to be crushed by an oncoming tank. The other options, having his leg or arm blown off and being unable to work or be productive, were even less welcome. Even after they told him about the mines, the army and the other villagers still needed him, and so Andreas pedaled his bike across roads and fields, avoiding airplanes and lone men. He knew he could die at any moment.

He was determined to help. Each day he made his way carefully through fields with his packages of instructions to the other Saxon wagons and army units. He rode into villages where people still worked as labourers even though the bombs fell, the fields were mined, and the miles of barbed wire ran heavy. His family needed money. Andreas was grateful when he received his first pay, but he felt that it was minuscule compared to the danger he faced each time he set out. He pedaled hard each day and he knew that he was only kept safe by some higher power.

When the war ended, he was relieved to learn that he would no longer have to face this sort of danger. He does not recall how he learned of Germany's surrender; he was simply told he did not have to do any more assignments for the army or anyone else.

From there, after the war was over, he worked as a labourer and found that while the money was good he could make more if he moved. His eldest sister was living in Canada now, but he had not seen her in sixteen years. He wondered if he should write to her. He did, and she responded. He could come to Canada; she would sponsor him[56].

He never imagined that he would need to go to a prison in order to get to Canada. That is what this holding camp felt like. Once his sister sponsored him, Andreas stayed in a big building along with all the other men his age. There they ran tests to assess his health. They questioned him for days about his German beliefs, and he told them everything about his life in the village and during the evacuation. He told them that he was not a part of the army. They coldly informed him that some more officials would look into things. Finally, they told him he could board a ship; he was going to Canada.

It seemed as if everyone on the boat, including himself, was seasick. The constant rocking motion drove him nearly mad, he recalls, but he still wanted to help, and as he had done when he volunteered to carry messages during the war, he did his part by making sure that the people knew where they were allowed to go on the ship. Some places were only for crew and others were only for passengers with tickets. He adapted quickly and he learned how to walk when the waves rocked the boat, and he recalls appreciating the beauty of the huge icebergs that they sailed past. He loved the first view of the new land he would come to love after nearly two weeks on the ship.

In Canada, he learned a new language, English, and he felt that it was as complex and irrational as Romanian. He learned it well, and he enjoyed the camaraderie of his sister and her family. He did not enjoy the heat of the sun, and he missed the climate of Transylvania. He worked in sandy tobacco farms to repay his sister for the cost of the sea voyage and sponsorship fees.

Later he moved into town, and he met the woman who became his beloved wife. They had two children. Later in life, he even learned woodworking. Now it offers a respite from the mundane routine of retirement. His children live in the area and he can see his grandchildren. He involves himself, as much as he can, in keeping the traditions of the Saxons alive.

Some days it seems like a lost cause, and no one really cares. They want action, adventure, and travel; they do not seem to have a sense of duty and loyalty to the past or an understanding of traditions and family. Andreas raises his voice now. His family holds on to these traditions.

He misses his immediate family. His mother and sisters are dead now, and he was the youngest child, but he keeps going unsure if it is by his own tenacity or because he still has much more to give.

Now he begins to tell me about some of the traditions that the farmers followed in Transylvania. Did I know that it was a group effort to work the land? I tell him, I know it now, thanks to him.

What about the history-makers in Transylvania? Do I know about the Saxons who helped create some of the best-known products? Yes, I reply. You mentioned Lysol? Correct! You can almost see his grin forming, but he will not grin and I know this.

He says, at least I have told my story. The traditions of my people need to be remembered. I am only one man. He smiles wanly. Not only a man, I reply, you are an inspiration.

The Long Way To Another Home

They need to debate the fate that they might face if they venture closer. There is no other way. Martin is not sure if the end of his life will be painful, but in that moment he feels certain he would never see his mother again. He is angry. These Americans would kill him on sight, and they would never understand that he is just a boy. He had heard that the Russians killed with impunity but the Americans were worse. That was why they fought the Germans. He takes a deep breath and decides that he will go on and head to Germany, to his family. His is the deciding vote.

With another deep breath, he begins to tell the other two what he is thinking. They must continue onwards. He fears losing his life, but he also will not lose hope. He knows his choice, his only choice. He feels sure he is going to die.

Martin grins and wiggles in his chair. He hates sitting down. He wants to do something; to walk, or to repair the deck, or to show some pictures. He has a lot of them, and he wants to show them to people, as many as he can. He also wants to share some of his memories, but first his wife must act as hostess. She asks what each person would like to eat and drink. Then she smiles and tells Martin to make his story to the point and not to pause to show pictures. He asks her to repeat herself. Photos, what photos? Please repeat yourself. She tells him again and he asks her to repeat herself. She glances his way, and then she tells him either to turn up his hearing aid, or to stop pretending he cannot hear her.

He smiles when she walks out of the room shaking her head. He leans back into the couch and looks around before asking, what part of his life is interesting? From the look on his face, I know he wants some sort of an answer, but...

He answers the question himself; a sly grin spreads across his face. There was that long walk, though. And the bombings – nothing serious, he says. And he did not see his parents for a few years. Moving from Transylvania to a new home in Germany and then to Canada. He smiles at the looks of amazement spreading over his listeners' faces. He tells us, put your little feet up and he will give us an outline of his life.

He stands up and walks to a photo album. He begins by showing pictures of his grandmother and aunts and uncles, then a picture of his parents. He comments how young his mother looks. He muses at how young his mother was at the time of his birth; after he left for the army, she had his baby sister, who is sixteen years younger than he is. He misses her and her smile, but he knows that she is in a better place. His parents did what they had to do to help him survive.

He was small as a child, but now he towers over every-one except for his nearly six-foot-tall grandson. His life had always been that of a farmer and of his wife's *entire* family, *he* was the only one who farmed once he arrived in Canada. His wife points out that her father had a nearly three-acre plot of land. In the city, Martin retorts. Martin's was fifty acres, a real farm. He tells everyone he has come a long way, literally. As he begins placing the photos back in its albums and on the shelves, he starts his story.

In the early fall of 1929, a small baby was born in his parents' home. The little boy was a welcome addition to the family, but his parents worried over his small size. He was smaller than his brothers and sisters were when they were born. He would grow strong, the midwife declared to his mother, but it would take him some time. Since Martin was so small, there was some fear he might not survive. There was no doctor in the village of

Pintak. The fees for a doctor were expensive, and farmers often did not have that amount of money. Martin did thrive, but he was the smallest child his age. At four weeks old, the family had him baptized in the small stone church in the center of Pintak.

Once the service was over, Martin's father stood up and proudly announced that, as host of this day, it was his pleasure to invite them to the family's home for a celebratory dinner. His family was of the Lutheran faith since the time of the Reformation, and a baptism was a special event for them that needed to be both acknowledged and celebrated.

The celebratory dinner acknowledged three things: the arrival of the new baby, the health of mother and child, and the new baby's baptism. The guests of honour were Martin's godparents and the village Pastor. The family prayed for the good health of the baby and everyone commented how healthy and strong Martin seemed. Years later, his mother told him that the table groaned under the weight of all the food. The oak table was large, and Martin could not believe her. This would be the last family gathering at the home of his parents for a while. Soon Martin would be on the move.

The village that Martin lived in faced an outbreak of typhoid[57]. Many villagers fell ill, and some of the older people died. His parents, fearing that they might lose their son, looked to his grandparents for help. For his protection, and to keep him healthy Martin's parents sent him to live with them for a time. His grandparents lived on the outskirts of Pintak where the disease had not struck. They also had a well near to their home that they had not built near the village creek. A connection to the creek meant that the well could be contaminated, and even if he went to his grandparents he could still contract the disease. Martin grew close to his grandparents, in particular to his grandmother. He also found a playmate in an aunt who was not much older than he was. Once the danger passed, Martin returned to his parents' house, and was grateful for the time he could now spend with his mother. He missed her presence when he stayed with his grandparents.

By the age of four, his mother taught him many things at home. She taught him how to care for the small animals the family owned: the chickens and the rabbits. The best thing she taught him was how to care for the small vegetable garden behind the family's house. He learned to take care in watering the tomatoes and to cover them if the weather turned cold. Martin loved the outdoors; he loved the sounds of the birds chirping in the trees, he loved the wind whipping his hair, and he loved the feel of the earth in his hands. He took every opportunity to work and play in the soil that he could. This was all a part of growing up to be a farmer. He recalls that no matter how dirty he made his shirt, his mother got it pristine white again.

Even farmers could do other things than simply farm and little Martin soon found a passion for woodworking. He loved watching the men in the workshop create chairs and tables and additions to houses of the village for growing families. He loved the smell of the fresh cut wood, and the brightly coloured paints fascinated him. He carefully held the wood planes, the saws, and the levels that the men gave him. He remembered how each man told him that it was important to think, take time, and check everything before taking any actions. They told him that once he was old enough, they would teach him more. For now, he could stay and watch – if he remained quiet.

There would be other challenges; he would turn five that year and school would begin soon. His teacher adored music, and it was an integral part of school. Martin was not musically inclined and shy, so he did not like to sing or to try to dance. School was the place where the children learned practical skills: reading and writing. It was the responsibility of the parents to correct any problems, behavioural or otherwise. Martin earned good marks and did not cause any problems for his parents or teacher. To him the worst punishment was to stay indoors peeling potatoes or being forced to write lines while his friends played outdoors. As he grew older, the two places he preferred to be in his spare time were outdoors and in the wood shop.

The summer of 1940 began with something new; Pintak and the rest of Northern Transylvania became a part of Hungary. It was not as big of an issue to him in comparison to other people in the village. In school, this meant that he would learn Hungarian and not Romanian. Martin recalls that he was more concerned about learning a new language.

His marks in Hungarian were good and his father was pleased. His mother told him that she expected him to do well, and he did. Since his marks showed that he had done his schoolwork well, his parents gave him permission to have fun with his friends after the teacher dismissed the class. He also helped around the house and kept his eye on the budding wheat and corn. His mother also wanted him to help care for the chickens and the horses. He wanted to go and be in the wood yard where he could help the older men with the basic repairs of chairs and other small wooden furniture. His parents agreed that Martin could play with his friends and help in the wood yard if he cleaned out the chicken coop each morning.

In the evenings when there was no more work to be done, the villagers of Pintak often held dances or got together to sing songs. Since he was an introverted young boy, this was not his favourite activity. Try as she might, his mother could not convince Martin to sing or dance. He felt that he could not sing and that he was not coordinated enough to dance. He also did not like to wear his special Sunday clothes, which he found to be a bit frilly. He was never allowed to get a single spot on the white shirt or black pants. Despite all of this, he still joined in the Pintak events. He wanted to spend time with the men who would talk in the corner, but he noticed something odd: the men would hush when he and other boys came close.

At the age of nine, Martin did not understand what might be worrying these men. He overheard them talk about a man called Adolf Hitler and about his abilities as a leader in Germany.

He heard about two countries, Germany and Austria, becoming one. His teacher showed them many maps, so he had a general idea of where these countries were. He heard that Hungary craved more land. Men from Greater Germany arrived in Pintak and other villages and Martin noticed that many people in the village became concerned. The men ignored the younger boys, but they were very interested in speaking with their older brothers, fathers and uncles.

Martin knew better than to ask more questions of the village men. He simply smiled and said nothing, but his brown eyes saw the fear in their faces. He remembers how he tried to work harder and better at school in an effort to make his parents smile at home more.

He did not yet understand that war could destroy everything the Saxons worked so hard to build. For him, war and violence happened in the past and one learned about them in history lessons. He believed it would not happen now. He felt that no matter what happened, he would be safe as long as he followed along and never ask too many questions; that was the best way to learn. He and the other boys did not look to the past, for they were too young to understand that the past influences the present and the future. He knew that some of his friends believed that the past would not repeat itself and that if Germany was strong once again, then there would be no war.

He recalls that the men in the wood shop also talked about Poland[58]. They debated in the evenings about the man who began a fight there and was trying to take back territory that Germany lost in a past war. He was not sure why the villagers were so concerned. In his lessons at school, the teacher taught the class that Germany and Austria lost much territory and dignity after the First World War. He did not give the class many details but he pointed out that losing power often meant lasting anger grew in the population.

Martin asked his parents about the Saxons. He wanted to know what happened to them after the end of the First World

War. He recalls that his mother began to cry, and his father told him that land and pride were lost, and there were now higher taxes and less food than there once was. Martin understood that it was hard for his father to talk about those events since he seemed to leave the room with tears in his eyes. He let the matter be. No harm would come to him, his father and mother repeated to him. He believed that they knew best and that they would all be safe.

No matter how hard the parents in the village tried to keep knowledge of world events away from their children, the children still found out. The adults in Pintak would talk about the subject, but as soon as the children came near, they would end the conversation or change the subject. Sometimes, though, people did not take notice if a person did not come into the room but was already there, and Martin often sat so quietly that even his parents did not notice him. They talked about France and Germany.

In June of 1940, they talked about Germany and a great victory they won. Martin finally gathered his courage and asked his grandparents about it. They told him that France and Germany fought, and Germany won and gained territory from France. This victory made up for the loss in the last war. Martin was happy that people were not fighting. His grandfather cautioned him not to assume anything. For now, though, he should not worry; he was a boy and his parents would need him soon. The harvest season was coming and Martin could be a big help to them.

Martin recalls he was never sure if it was the importance of the event or because now he was older, but his parents told him the news right away. On 30 August 1940, Hungary, an ally of Greater Germany, regained a portion of Transylvania from Romania, and their village was part of that territory. Pintak was now a part of Hungary[59]. It was all part of something greater, and his parents and many other people did not know yet how this would directly affect the village. They assured him that they loved him and reminded him that he needed to be a good, strong, and obedient boy. Things would be all right and that he needed to trust that God would provide for them all. Martin accepted this without comment. He remembers that he had many questions, but he knew better than to ask anything. Besides, his parents would not tell him any more even if he asked.

The beginning of 1941 brought new challenges. This was his final year of school and he did not enjoy the time he spent in class as much as he had in the past two years. He did not enjoy learning the Hungarian language much, and he found that it was harder to learn than Romanian was. Martin was not happy because that meant he would need to study later in the evenings. He recalls that he did not appreciate learning other languages until many years later. He decided, though, that if the teacher wanted the students to do this then there must be an important reason for the request. Each night he sat on the chair in the kitchen and read from the school lesson book that he wrote in during classes each day. He wanted excellent marks at the end of the school year so that his father could not complain about a lack of studying on his part. If he failed his course, his father would worry about whether or not he could handle other responsibilities.

In May, Martin began to notice that his father and grandfather had long discussions about a country that he knew about only from maps and short mentions in his classroom. Germany and Hungary were attacking this country called Russia, and it was close to Hungary. He did not understand why there needed to be more fighting since Germany was still attacking Britain. His father attempted to dismiss his worries by saying that Britain would surrender to mighty Germany, and he should trust the announcements that they heard over the radio.

Martin saw, though, that his father did not seem convinced that this new attack was the right thing to do. He remembers that his father thought long and hard before saying each word. It seemed as if he worried that someone might misinterpret what he said. His father told him to keep his peace and look around the village. He should be careful about asking too many questions, and he should pay attention to things that were happening in the village. Martin found his father's instructions to be confusing, but he decided that they seemed important, and he would follow them. He also felt that the summer would be more fun with the hint of a mystery.

Martin decided to look for that mystery. He recalls how amazed he was to notice that there were men in the village that he did not recognize and at first, he thought that they were Romanians or Hungarians until they spoke in German but not Saxon. He saw that the village men tried to avoid the newcomers or would speak to them in formal tones. Some of the younger boys would go up and talk to the strangers at length. Martin asked his father if these people were the reason for his recent caution. His father told him, yes and that Martin should be careful to listen and not speak.

His father asked him what else he noticed. Martin thought for a while and said the dances were different and there were new songs that talked about Germany and its might. He was not sure if he liked them. His father told him to keep his feelings and opinions closely guarded; he was young and the new men might be interested in those feelings. They were from the Nazi party and they were here to recruit men to fight on Germany's side in the war. Martin was happy that they never paid much attention to him or the other young boys, though on some Sundays they wanted the boys to go out marching through the village instead of going to church.

Summer gave him the opportunity to enjoy the warmth of the sun, and his mother and grandmother let him run with his friends if he finished all of his chores first. He helped his friends build forts and many of them asked for his advice; they all seemed to know that he could do a good job and had a talent for building. Martin felt humbled that his friends felt this way about him and that they placed their faith in his abilities. He spent more time in the fields helping with weeding and became proficient at not getting his hands burnt when he pulled out nettles. He also spent more time in the wood shop asking the workers a few questions, and now some of the men appreciated that his questions were thoughtful and he only asked them when he needed to.

Martin recalls that some of the older boys still teased him saying that because he was still small for his age, he would keep them all out of trouble – most people thought he was younger than his 12 years. He remembers that when he was with the group and the boys did get into trouble, the punishments were not always as harsh. Perhaps this was because Martin was quiet and, although the villagers knew his age, they did not think that a well-behaved boy would get into any trouble.

Confirmation and the end of his childhood were approaching quickly. On Palm Sunday in 1943, he faced a public examination in the church, and he needed to answer questions about doctrine and faith correctly. He did not look forward to it because he did not like speaking in public, but he prepared for it with as much diligence as he could. He reread Luther's small catechism, for he knew that the Pastor would ask questions from it. To his delight, when the day came and the Pastor began to ask questions, he knew the answers. After the service, he and his family went back to his house for a meal that his mother and grandmother prepared. He remembers that most of the food served by the family they did not eat on ordinary days because of the time it took to prepare and the loss of money. Butchering a pig meant that they would not be able to sell that animal in the fall and have the money to pay their taxes.

The planting season passed quickly and so did summer.

After Martin's confirmation, he joined the village's boys club. All the confirmed and unmarried boys could join and participate. They organized and hosted dances and singing events. He talked with the boys and danced with the girls of the village. He tried to make himself feel older by telling the girls that he would leave for the army soon. His father was fond of reminding him that he had to wait until he was twenty-one for that to happen, and that was still many years away. Martin imagined that after serving in the army, he would return to Pintak and most likely marry one of the village girls. He was happy to find that his friends who were confirmed with him and others who were some years older had much in common with him and they did have fun, except in a different way from when they were all young boys. They now talked about the same subject as the other men: the war.

He still went regularly to the carpentry workshop in the village. Along with the chairs and tables for family kitchens, they also built and repaired items for the church. The wooden pews were old and needed much care. Martin remembers that they would make sure that the bottoms of the legs were strong so that the villagers of Pintak could sit on them safely. He remembers that he liked how one particular man showed him how to measure the pieces of wood and how to keep them level. When putting two pieces of wood together he taught Martin it was important that they fit well, otherwise the whole piece of furniture could weaken and break. Martin found that this bit of advice was a good metaphor for everyday life since he needed to take care in everything he did. He also learnt the value of listening more carefully.

In July, his father told him the unpleasant news that Russia and Germany were at war. Martin could not understand why there should be a war on that front since Hungary and Germany were already fighting against Yugoslavia. His father did not say that Hungary was also fighting against Russia, but Martin felt that since Hungary was an ally with Germany and that the men would be called from the villages to lend their support. He looked at the copies of maps that he drew from the ones in the schoolroom, and he saw that Russia was not far from Hungary. He felt that the best way to keep his father from worrying was to not ask many questions. Martin saw that his father relaxed once word came over the radio in the Pintak hall that Germany had gained victories against the Russian Army. Martin hoped that this would mean no more war and no more hardships.

Martin knew that his father feared that, since he was still not an old man, he might have to go to Russia as a soldier.[60]. His father remembered the First World War and the impact of the Treaty of Versailles. He spoke to Martin about the dangers of war and how it might affect their family. He told Martin to be strong and brave and to trust in God. Martin knew that his family worried, but he saw how his father smiled more when the Germans won some victories. Although he never said it, Martin felt that perhaps if the Germans would win more victories, then the Russians would surrender and there would be peace. Martin decided to think positively, and he turned his attention to something more important: the harvest.

For much of the harvest season, the word from the Russian front was good. Martin also heard that the German army and its allies, Hungary and Italy, had won victories against the Yugoslavian Army. However, Russia and its vast land took its toll on the German army and they began to suffer defeats. This meant the war would go on longer. It also meant that soon, the villagers of Pintak would be asked to give more to the Hungarian Army. His father worried more and spoke about the dangers ahead, but he encouraged his family to always trust in God, for he would provide. Martin loved his father's faith and he felt that his father knew what was best for the family. He told Martin to concern himself with the beginning of school and keeping the school warm. There were not enough young boys in the class now to fetch wood and tend the stove, so the teacher asked the young men in the village club for help.

The war seemed to be at the top of everyone's mind, and Martin recalls that everyone said that they supported the German army and its leadership, but in that praise, there was always a sense of hesitancy. The younger men who would leave soon to serve in the army talked only about Russia, specifically that they did not want to fight there. Martin noticed that the men from Germany were nearly always in the hall and taking notes. Some of the older boys and men were called over to talk with them. There was a tension in the village that he could neither understand, nor express. When he asked his father about it, his father said it was because the men from Germany wanted everyone to support their cause whatever the cost. Saxon men who were deemed fearful or troublesome were censured. Martin's father never mentioned what they were told, but Martin remembers that, over time, many of the men who were usually more outspoken did not talk much now unless they were in a private home. Martin began to understand that observing people was good, and he should not discuss his observations with people he did not trust.

Although the new men tried to tell everyone that the Germans would gain a great victory, privately his father told the family that not a single man in the village believed them, but they publically agreed with the strangers. His father cautioned everyone in the family to guard his or her remarks when they were in public, and he told Martin to observe and not speak. Martin was now at the age when these Nazi men would want something from him, and possibly try to poison his mind, his father told him. They needed young boys to help them now that most of the men were gone, and Martin was the perfect age. The radio announcers told a different story than the visiting men: peace was not close. Martin prayed that good news would come next year.

He wondered when his father would need to leave for the army, and he worried about it. He recalls that he tried to ignore and bury his fears with the many activities that the village had; dances, singing, church, and work, but he knew that the war was pushing his carefree days aside. Along with the other boys in the group, he wondered what the future held. He worried about the year to come.

He has good memories of the Advent and Christmas season of 1943. There was singing but no dances, which was fine because he was not an enthusiastic dancer. He spent many days in the house working on repairs with his father. In the woodshed, he built his mother a small chest to put her needles and yarn into for Christmas. When he gave it to her, her eyes shone, and she smiled and told him she was thankful that he built such a nice chest for her. He enjoyed Christmas and the food that the family ate. He decided that this was a good ending to the year.

The announcements coming from the radio were more worrisome, though. He was not sure what it all meant, and he knew now that the last war claimed many Saxon lives and much of their farmland was taken away. He did not know what difference this war would make to his life's plans. He wanted to be a farmer, and he decided that no matter how this war ended, he would still be a farmer. He heard about increasing losses for the German forces and about the advancing Russian troops. He could see many of his friends dismissed any positive spin that the radio announcer put on the news. According to the announcer, even though Germany suffered some defeats, the Russians were suffering more and graver ones. This always produced a shrug or coughing fits from some men. Martin knew that it was their only way of disagreeing with the announcements out loud. He tried to concentrate on making little shelves and other practical items for people in the village, and he talked with his father about repairing the stables outside their home. He tried to avoid talking about the war, and he did not want to consider what might happen.

Although he tried to concentrate on more work in both the fields and the wood shop, Martin was aware that the announcements about the war took on a more negative tone. The radio announcer no longer made mention of victories. He talked about troop movements; they seemed to be moving closer to Pintak. Martin loathed the idea that the Russians might harm his family or land. It would turn out that he did not need to worry because the German Army retreated sooner than expected.

In September 1944, the radio announcer told the Saxon people across all of Northern Transylvania that they must evacuate[61] – they only had a few days to prepare. The German and Russian Armies would be coming soon. Martin helped pack the most important belongings that the family needed. Food, some clothes, and livestock were all that they could take. He wanted to bring some wood and the chest he made, but his father told him no. He didn't argue, but he didn't share how he felt either. He helped to load the wagons and supplies for the horses as quickly as possible. Within a few days everything was ready. The Saxon villagers assembled and the Pastor prayed for the protection of them all.

They certainly needed protection. Martin recalls that it did not matter if the evacuees were Germans or not. If airplanes from any of the fighting forces saw wagon columns or intact railways, they dropped bombs. He would run and duck under a wagon or a bush to protect himself, oftentimes hearing the bullets hit the ground beside him. He hid his face to protect his eyes from the dirt and shrapnel. He despised the sounds of planes. When he saw that people got hurt and could not walk, he realized that it did not matter to the people in the planes if those on the ground were refugees or army. He needed to run and hide as fast as he could. The train of wagons would often travel at night, and the trip took about seven weeks.

The wagons moved more slowly than a walking pace because the roads were rough, so his family could not stop for long. They walked for as many miles each day as they could and then they rested with the horses for a few hours. People took turns sleeping in a corner of the moving wagon. Since they spent so much time walking, the trip seemed to be less fun than Martin had hoped. He wanted to see some of the places that he read about in his history books, but he only saw burnt homes, dirt, mud, and destruction everywhere. They travelled through

Hungary and when they reached Austria, he heard rumours that people could return to their villages, but his parents decided not to go back. They heard that the land they owned for centuries was now in the hands of Romanians.

It saddened Martin that his family would not return to Pintak, but he tried to think positively that everyone was safe. He wondered where they might live, and what they might do in their new home. He wished he had more skills in woodworking and farming, then he would not be a simple day labourer in the fields. He believed that soon, though, he would gain the skills he needed. He strongly hoped that the army would not call on him, but he heard rumours that the army was looking for young men and older boys to help defend German held territories. At least he hoped that this was the case.

However, the army did need him. At the age of 15, he left his parents, and as much as this seemed like a great adventure for him, he missed them very much. He was with hundreds of other young boys, and Martin recalls learning how to march and to shoot a rifle. He hoped that these would never be necessary skills for him, and he thinks that it was because he hoped that the war would be over soon. The people who trained them told the boys often that they were in service for Germany to save it. Some of the boys were excited about this prospect, but Martin was unsure. He recalls feeling glad when word came in 1945 that the war was over, but he was now far away from his family, and he was determined to reunite with them.

Martin received letters while he was in the training camp, so he learned that his family were heading to Germany[62]. He knew two other boys, Peter and Philip, from Pintak who had been recruited along with him. Together they decided that Germany was not a long walk away, and that they could get there in a reasonable time. Martin recalls that he did not understand how far it was. His footwear was almost new; he had received a pair of army boots when he began his training. He was not pleased that the only clothes he had now were some farming clothes and a uniform. His uniform was brown and he recalls that parts of it needed to be pulled off, especially any symbols of the Nazi party, otherwise it might call attention to him and his friends.

After packing some meagre foodstuffs and extra clothes in a large wooden chest, the three of them began to walk. Martin recalls that none of them had a map. They decided that they would walk towards the last place they knew that their parents had lived. The first night, they stopped in a field. The older boys told him not to light a fire since there might be animals or dangerous things that could find them if they saw any light. Martin thought at first that they meant bears or other large animals. He recalls that in the middle of the night he woke up suddenly thinking that the boys really meant soldiers. He did not want to think about what might happen to the three of them if they met up with soldiers.

He was curious to see what the men from America looked liked, and he had heard that their values were not the same as the Germans. He did not think highly of how they might treat German soldiers that they caught. He cannot remember now what made him think that, but he does recall that during the training he was often told that he would prefer death to capture. He hoped that they would not cross paths with soldiers from any side. The boys continued to walk, but they were careful because there were landmines and unused artillery shells in the fields. They hoped to be in Germany soon.

Martin was satisfied that the walk was going mostly as planned. By day they walked. By night they slept.

Martin recalls that they were nearing the border when they saw tanks and soldiers. To his horror, he saw that they were not German; they were American soldiers, and they were heading towards a compound of sorts. Martin was not sure what it was. The other boys were equally distraught. He recalls the heated conversation the three of them had when they discussed what they should do next.

Philip was the first to speak and suggested they go back – towards Transylvania or west to Hungary. Peter insisted they continue on towards their parents and Germany. When Martin agreed with Peter, Philip declared he would not speak with either of them again if this decision lead their capture, imprisonment or injury. No one mentioned death.

They continued to walk towards the camp. Martin recalls that one of the men spotted the three boys and motioned them to come over. From up close, Martin could see that it was indeed a military camp. The barbed wire and gates told him as much. The soldiers had guns and demanding voices. One of them pointed to where Martin and his friends were coming from. With a mix of curiosity and trepidation, they walked forward. One of the soldiers walked up to the boys. Martin recalls that he looked closely at all three of them, but especially at him. It seemed as if he was trying to make up his mind about something.

The soldier began to speak in English, a language Martin could not understand. Once the soldier saw that none of the boys seemed to know what he said, he motioned them to leave. With relief, they walked away.

Martin turned back to look at the compound. He saw people inside. They all seemed thin, and he wondered what was wrong with them. They seemed unhappy and all wore gray clothes. He remembers a feeling of such despair coming from them. It was only later that he found out that it was a concentration camp[63]. He was furious when he learned that this was what the Germans did to unwanted people. He was proud to be a Saxon, and he did not want to be associated with the German Third Reich.

His thoughts went back to his family. He feared that they were dead. When he mentioned this to Philip and Peter, they voiced the same worries about their own families. Would they be hurt, or worse? Martin was not ashamed to be a Saxon, but since he was a German, he felt betrayed by the leaders of the Nazi party; they had promised to create something better[64].

He wanted to find some answers, but he recalls that all he found now was more questions. He wanted to fight someone or something, but slowly his anger faded and he continued his journey toward his parents.

Martin recalls that after many weeks they reached the border of West Germany. He was grateful that they were safe, and he learned that his family was on the border of Austria and Germany, so he was still far away from them. He decided to stay where he was, and he found work as a farm hand. He hoped that he would make enough money to find his family and be with them. Over time, he was able to regain contact with them through friends from Pintak who worked with him or lived close to him. He heard that his mother had delivered another child, this time a girl, and Martin was very happy about this news.

He decided to remain in Germany because there was work and food there, and from the reports from Romania, that the land the Saxons once had was appropriated by the Romanians as abandoned land. He was bitter about this because his childhood dream was to farm there, but he accepted that life was unfolding differently than he envisioned. He remained in Germany for several years, until he was 22 and then, after continuous letters between him and a cousin living in Canada he decided to immigrate there in 1951.

The decision was made, but the process took longer than he anticipated. Since he was a German-speaking person, he needed to complete questionnaires before immigrating. Once his answers satisfied the Canadian officials, he boarded a boat to Canada. The trip took two weeks, and Martin recalls that these were the worst two weeks of his life, and he vowed solemnly that he would never set foot on a boat again.

When he was able to run off the boat, he took a train to his new home where his cousin lived. The next day his cousin took him to a farm where he would work. Along the way, Martin and his cousin passed by an elderly couple who were wearing a familiar ethnic costume. His cousin pointed them out to him saying that these people were also new to the country. Martin dismissed them because he had a more pressing interest. The farm where he would have his first job in Canada neared. As he talked with the farmer, his cousin went inside the house.

In a matter of minutes, the farmer's wife called to him to come inside. The people Martin saw walking on the road knew his cousin, and they wanted to meet him. He walked into the house to meet with two lively people. Their names were Philip and Rosina, and to his amazement, they were younger than his cousin made them out be. They insisted that he should come to a dance the next evening where they and their young daughters would be attending as well. He accepted their invitation.

When he walked into the dance, he felt that he was once again back home in Pintak. People were singing and laughing, and best of all they were speaking in Saxon. He was introduced to a wonderful girl, Hilda, the daughter of the same couple who invited him to the dance. She was young and full of laughter, and even though his was a quiet personality, her zest for life was a compliment to his own soft-spoken personality. They enjoyed each other's company and romance blossomed.

They married in 1953, the family grew with the birth of a daughter, Geri, in 1954, and then there were two sons, Eric and Richard. Their youngest, Liz, was born in 1966. During that time, Martin and his wife constantly moved from one house to another but he had stable work in a factory where he used his practical math skills and earned the respect of his peers and supervisors.

He bought a farm when his children were young; it was not large – about fifty acres. He loved being there. He loved work-ing the land because it gave him a sense of connection to life back in Transylvania. He continued to work at the factory, and he enjoyed his ever-growing brood of nieces and nephews. His family, some of his sisters at least, came to Canada later, and he finally had the chance to meet his youngest sister.

Later, and with regret, he decided to move once more. He loved the farm, but he admits that he needed to move. It was in his blood. They moved to a lovely cabin near a lake. There Martin found a peaceful setting, where he could have his family nearby and he could make all the repairs he cared to. His love of woodworking and renovating their home admittedly annoyed his wife, but he enjoyed it, and she would grudgingly tell him that she liked the improvements once the projects were complete.

After a few years there, they moved back to the city where Martin settled into a routine, and a very small condominium. He was anxious to move again right away and they did, still in the city but into a house that he could fix and renovate. He likes to say that his wife is happy with all the moves, but he also says that moving is a bit of a strain now as they age.

He smiles, and asks me if there is anything he might have left out or if there was something I loved? I tell him, oh, the walk, the bombings, the people, you. He grins, and he begins to walk towards a desk. He pulls out some loose photos along with several oversized albums. He tells me that he has not finished showing me pictures. He has an entire lifetime to show. And with that, he sits down beside me and shows me more pictures of his life and his loves.

The Facts Are Not Ordinary

His brother loved that motorcycle. They loved riding together through hills around the town, but after the accident, Georg vowed he would never ride another motorcycle ever again. War was horrible, and in Budapest he saw the worst: men whose deaths were ignored, who rotted where they died. He hated the smell of death, the pungent, and awful, smell that he had hoped he would never smell again. Budapest haunted him. There were the friends whom he had just met who were now dead, or injured and left to die in the mud. Bombs, guns... and now this... the motorcycle at the side of the road draws his attention, the face is so familiar, and the shape of the body is as well.

It cannot possibly be his motorcycle. Anyone, Georg hopes, anyone else. He prays it is anyone but him, and if it is, then it is Georg's fault. He begins to think back to his own close brush with death...

Georg and his cousin have a friendly argument that has been ongoing for years; one says the other does not talk, and the other contends that he does. This time, his cousin might have a point; Georg is not going to tell me much, just the bare facts. Yet he finds himself recalling so many events in his life; the people that influenced him greatly, and those who left him too soon. There were some he cared for deeply, and some who simply influenced him by their very existence. That is a cryptic statement, I tell him. He assures me that he will explain.

Georg was born in the farming village of Oberneudorf in 1926. Since there was not a hospital nearby and the birth was not expected to be complicated, he was born with the help of a midwife. He believed his mother was wonderful and unique, more so than most, because she already had another child from another marriage, something that was rare in Oberneudorf. The midwife came to see the new baby and his mother each day for the next four weeks. After that, she did not come back, since she was sure that his mother could take care of the child and the house on her own now. Georg was a quiet baby who rarely cried. That soft-spoken nature is a trait that has stayed with him throughout his life.

Growing up in a farming village he had his share of challenges and duties. As a young boy, Georg would wake up early to do small tasks. He was responsible for cleaning the chicken coop and helping in the vegetable gardens. He did not enjoy collecting eggs because the chickens often pecked at him. He liked being outside and breathing the fresh air. To him, the best time was spent with friends, running through the meadows and down the road. Young Georg did all his work without much fuss, and he did not complain about his life.

In his mind, everyone needed to help and do their part, and so that is what he did. School started early for him. In Oberneudorf, the children began attending school at the age of five or six[65], and Georg remembers that he started classes when he was five. He did not find much to like about school, and he preferred to spend his time outside the classroom.

The only consolation was that all the boys and girls went to school. His teacher taught them German and Romanian, and Georg learned that his teacher was a Saxon man who took courses to be proficient in the Romanian language. His teacher also taught the class music and history. None of the subjects taught in class gave Georg any desire for more education; although he was intelligent enough that if he had wanted to, he could have continued and the family could afford to pay for it. He was happy to please his father and his mother.

Georg loved his mother, and she in turn encouraged him to learn. One winter, when Georg was nine, she took ill and did not get better. She died at the age of 28. The entire community came to pay their respects. It was traditional in Oberneudorf for the Saxon community to attend the funeral of someone from the village, but Georg believed she was unique; after all, she was his mother. At her funeral, beautiful and somber music played and she was laid to rest in the village cemetery. Georg is not entirely sure what she died of; he remembers his older half-sister telling him it was pneumonia.

He missed her terribly though, but knew that because he was a boy, he should not talk about his sadness. In Georg's village, life was like that; there was much work that needed to be done. Reflection was appropriate, provided one did not reflect for too long. Georg helped his father work on the farm, and he helped to bring in the harvests from the other village fields. He remembers that, as he grew older, more was expected of him, and he accepted these new responsibilities without argument. He also noticed that the atmosphere around him began to change: The men in his village now talked about things that were happening far away from Oberneudorf.

By the age of 12, in 1938, he recalls hearing that Hungary was being given a part of its former territory back and the news caused a lot of excitement in the village. Hungary gained territory from Czechoslovakia[66], and many people in Oberneudorf believed that they might be allowed more land back. Georg was not sure why the men believed this, and he did not think things would improve just because Oberneudorf was a part of Hungary. There were Germans in Hungary, and even the Saxons who lived in their villages for centuries and who owned land were still treated like outsiders.

He hoped for lasting peace – at least long enough so that he could grow old. Some believed it would last years, and others argued that Germany would keep gaining land but through peaceful means. Others argued that peace in the area – the Balkans, the place in which they lived – was something that would never last long. The men all remembered 1939 as the year that they worried the most for themselves and for those they loved. It did not happen all of a sudden; things became tense in September when news came of an attack in Poland. Some of the men who had families feared that if they were sent away, they might never return from any war between these countries. To others, it was a new adventure that everyone would begin.

Georg was not a person to ask many questions, and he simply waited and listened. What he overheard worried him; fighting had begun. At first, he thought it was happening in Romania, and then he heard that battle was actually taking place in the country called Poland. He was happy that it was not near his home otherwise people he loved might get hurt. Then he overheard that Germany might have to fight France and Britain. He hoped that this would not happen; from his history lessons, he knew what happened when both Germany and Austria-Hungary lost the last war. After that war, some territory was transferred to Romania, the Saxon people lost some of their lands, and now they paid more taxes.

He wondered what the next year would hold, but for now, he saw that some of the Oberneudorf men looked relieved. France and Britain did not start to fight, so there might not be a war after all.

Often, news from the outside world came through older lines of communication like word of mouth or telegrams from official government sources, but the farther the village was from a major city, the longer it took for the telegrams to arrive. Oberneudorf was up to date, and had a radio, too. This was how the village men learned about the fighting between France and Germany, and the victory that Germany won over the numerically-superior French army. Georg was told about these events, since the older men believed that at 14 he was old enough to understand what was happening, but this did not mean that the adults wanted his opinion, and Georg did not give it. The news did not matter to him because it did not change his life in any immediate way.

That November, the men seemed very excited, and debated the merits of some new leadership or past leadership. At first, Georg thought that they were having a heated discussion deciding who would sit on the council for the village, but he never remembered the men getting that passionate about it before. It was usually just agreeing on choices from the eldest, most capable, and smartest men of the village[67]. Then, they talked about the transfer of land and perhaps paying less tax. He worried that the Romanians were planning to take more land away from the village and how they might change the taxes. Then one of the men told him that Oberneudorf and the other surrounding villages, including the city of Bistritz, had been handed over to Hungary. Georg was not indifferent, but he was not as excited as most other people. He knew that power and land changed hands, but as with the defeat of France, he felt that it did not affect them in any noticeable way. He did not think that it ever would, really.

He enjoyed the time he spent with other young boys and the activities that they took part in together. He was not sure why a group of Nazis who arrived in the village wanted the boys to skip the church service on Sunday mornings to march and to sing songs about their love of everything German instead. Georg felt that he was German and a Transylvania Saxon; but more to the point, he wasn't from Germany. He saw how the people in the village reacted to these new men, and how careful people were now about verbalizing their feelings or opinions when they were outside the privacy of their homes. He joined in the marches and thought that some of the songs sounded nice. He mentioned this to his father, and his father pointed out that the words were more important. After that, Georg still sang the songs, but he also paid attention to the words. The summer went by, and soon would come the time to bring in the harvest. Georg looked forward to this. Other surprises might come, but for the moment, he looked forward to the harvest and more work.

Just before the harvest began, in 1941, there was an announcement on the radio: Germany was at war with Russia. The announcer also said that Italy and Hungary had also declared war on Russia in support of Germany. Georg felt some dismay at this news since this meant that there would be more fighting. The Hungarian Army took away some horses from the villagers earlier that year, right at the end of the planting season, and the harvest would be harder without them. He wondered when Hungary would declare war on Russia as well. He hoped that it would not happen, but when it did, he was not surprised. The Hungarian army would call for more horses, and this might mean that the village would be left to rely on oxen to pull the wagons during the harvest. He was now considered an adult – he had been confirmed into the Lutheran Church in 1940 – so he was expected to work and do his part without complaining, and he was growing up to be a strong, tall, blond-haired, blue-eyed young man.

His hopes of a quick German victory were dashed when he heard about the losses in Russia. Everyone around him seemed more worried, and they wondered if Russia might attack Hungary. The visiting Nazis assured the villagers that this was only a small setback, and that the might of the German Army was superior to that of the Russians. The German men reluctantly admitted that they and their allies were outnumbered, but this was also the case in France, and Germany had still defeated the French. The temperature in the mountains was dropping, and Georg could only wonder how cold it was in Russia. The men never described the climate there, and Georg decided it was best not to ask. His father did not say much either. Since Georg was so young, only 15, the army would not call for him. He wondered what would happen to him and his family, though, should the war continue to go badly for Germany.

He recalls that life under Hungarian rule was tense: There were fewer horses to help with the farm work, and although they paid fewer taxes, they were still high. He recalls the sense

of pride that he felt when he was able to help pay the family's
taxes; he was healthy, strong, and alive, and he could serve his
country. To Georg, it meant that in a small way, he was supporting the fight against the Russian Army, one in which many Saxon
men were already fighting far away in the land of white death —
a term which many villagers used when they talked about Russia.
He recalls that when he said this to some of the men of the village, he knew from the looks on their faces that he was being
idealistic. He did not think so, only that he was young, and perhaps by staying positive and working hard, he could show his
support.

The year 1942 brought more bad news. The announcements on the radio told of another invasion, this time from
the West. Seeing the faces of the men in the village go from
expressions of hope to despair drove home the realization that
Germany might lose this war. The Americans were now fighting against the Germans. Georg initially was shocked that the
American people would fight against Germany, and alongside
Russia. Soon his shock turned to fury. Germany did not do anything to America... Why did they decide to fight? He hoped that
Germany and its allies would win. Russia seemed to be a mass
of fighting men, and Georg feared that this would destroy his
home. He loved Oberneudorf, and he feared what the Russians
might do. He was thankful that Romania was closer to the border of Russia, and that Romania's allies could hold this vast army
from his village for a while. He did not say much to anyone
about either his hopes or fears.

He did not want to go to the hall to hear the news on the
radio, but he went anyway, mostly out of curiosity, but also in a
vain hope that the Germans and Hungarians had won the war,
and he would not have to leave his home. The Nazi party members were now speaking to him on a regular basis; he was nearly
16 and a strong man. He hated their attention, and he despised
the men and their constant intrusions in his life. If war came to
his home he would fight, but not before that time.

He tried to focus his thoughts on the harvest and planting, and doing what a good farmer does, but he recalls that he was too interested in the war news. He quickly made his way to the hall after his work was done to hear the daily radio announcements regarding the war. He was shocked to hear the voice of Hitler once, and he recalls how mesmerized everyone was by what Hitler said. Georg didn't believe in the man, and he feared that the war would continue to go badly no matter what this Hitler said.

As much as he longed for one more impressive victory for the German Army in Russia, there never was one. He recalls that this worry would haunt him for a long time. Russia's countless numbers weighted heavily on his mind, as loss after loss continued to happen to Germany and its allies. The Americans began to make their presence known along the French coastline. He recalls the excitement and fear that raced through him each evening before he heard the news report. As the Russians drew closer to their former borders, his thoughts turned to an undeniable fact: He might have to kill or be killed. There was only death on his mind from that point forward.

Georg brooded, and he made alternate plans for his life. First and foremost he planned to live and die in Oberneudorf, and failing that, to live and die in Transylvania. He knew that he did not want to die young, or without just cause, or anywhere other than in Transylvania. He refused to consider the possibility that he might die in Russia; he would not be a nameless number unmentioned in dispatch and in radio announcements. He had come to despise the Nazis and the men who supported this group and what they stood for, but he recalls that along with all the young boys of the village, he wanted to be a part of something bigger. He felt that he could support the German people but not the Nazi Party, since the Nazi's promises were not coming true. Germany, he mused, might see a victory someday, but it would not come soon. They were fighting a war on two fronts now, and he was intelligent enough to know that by doing this they had effectively handed themselves a defeat in a war that they were winning.

Georg hoped for the war to end. In many announcements, the number of dead or wounded were not mentioned. He recalls that the number of Russians who were dead was mentioned, millions of men and the many divisions of tanks, but he found the reports hard to believe given that they had such a large army. Based on the looks on the older men's faces, he understood that they remembered things he did not know about, and he suspected that the Germans would lose.

Like the other younger boys, Georg recalls that no matter how skeptical he might have been, he remained optimistic for a victory. As 1942 turned into 1943 with no stunning victory for Germany and its allies, his hopes faded[68]. Both the German Army and its Russian foes inched closer to Oberneudorf. He was in despair over the prospect of leaving his village and dying; it forced him to think about his mother who was taken away so young with so much life left. He loved her and missed her; her humor, and her confidence.

He recalls that his thoughts of her were never morbid, but rather bittersweet. The present often intruded upon his memories with the noises of planes overhead and trains traveling eastward. The sounds never seemed far off, and Georg knew that soon the armies would be in Romania – far too close for his liking. He overheard one of the more vocal members of the Nazi Party, a Helmut, commenting on his age and how he would make a fine soldier. Georg was 17 now, and this man, whom Georg felt sure would never see action, wanted him to fight[69]. He decided to consider service in the army, for there were worse things that could happen to him. He recalls that he must have been thinking aloud because one day a man, he cannot recall when or who this was, commented to him that he should consider service to the Motherland. He thought the suggestion was preposterous; he did not want to fight for the Nazis… but he could fight for his home, and he was old enough to do so. His father seemed to accept the idea, and he had a younger half-brother, so Georg knew the family name would survive even if he did not. Of course, he also wanted to survive, and he felt that the longer he was a part of the army and the more senior an officer he could become, the safer he might be; that meant he needed to leave now.

By 1944, the war was turning against the Nazis, and Georg was in the army. He was sent to Budapest. At first, he thought it was good to be closer to home, but soon he realized that it was nothing more than a death trap filled with guns, shots, blood, and gore. The screams of injured men and the stench of death were all around him. Too often, the blood of comrades-in-arms would splatter on his uniform. The horrible screams of horses and the men trying to calm them haunted his dreams; he had heard horses scream when they were injured in the village and it was happening a lot now. Even when he slept, there was no peace. He hid in bombed-out homes, and he prayed that the bombs would not send him to oblivion.

By the end, he did not care. He hardly ate; there were few rations to go around, and even less time to eat them. The Russians inched closer, and the armies of Hungary and Germany fought on. Georg believed he was destined for a horrible death in the middle of the streets of Budapest.

He found that his best companion was the gun he had. He kept his wits about him, but death attacked every person in the city of Budapest. Not once could he let his guard down. As the Russians advanced and the Germans pulled back, the fighting grew fiercer. It seemed as if the German and Hungarian armies would fight for every inch of ground that they still held.

The German soldiers did not pull out or retreat. Their commanding officers ordered them to stay in their positions longer than a sane man should have[70]. Georg began to forget the days, for they passed all the same way: fighting, ducking for cover, shooting back, and killing. He forgot that he wanted to be a farmer; he just wanted to survive. He heard that the army was going to blow up the bridges linking Buda to Pest, and it was a scramble to get across them before this happened. before this happened. Those who did not make it fought a losing battle to stay alive. There was no quarter given to anyone.

He recalls to this day the sound of the bridges blowing up behind him and a hopeless feeling that he would die. His certainty about his fate was mirrored in the eyes of the rest of the men in his unit. Still, his company was ordered to remain in Budapest. He despaired that he would never have a life beyond the gray walls of the city. His ears filled with the roars of cannons and machine guns and the whistling bombs from planes overhead. Both armies were intent on sending all the soldiers and civilians to their deaths. He was slow to realize that he had his part in this madness, but recalls that at the time, his goal was to survive – nothing more.

Georg knew that his chances of surviving diminished each day. The war carried on and so did he; he was still sure that he would die. Each street seemed the same, gray tombs of buildings, and hidden inside them were snipers, and landmines. He was determined not to be a casualty. He saw that injured men were not treated, but they were left where they lay in the hopes that fellow comrades would have pity on them and treat their injuries. This did not happen often; when things got worse, compassion was never given.

Georg recalls that so many of the men were hungry, or at least they said they were. He also recalls that while he never was starving, he did lose weight. He wanted to focus on the end of the war, but in Budapest, that hope was a thing of the past. There was only that minute or this hour, depending on where he was situated; if he daydreamed, he would be a prime target for snipers. It did not matter which side shot him, he would be dead. They haunted the place, and to him they were nothing more than parasites determined to suck the remaining hope from the lives of the other men.

Even the people who were Germans but were snipers had that same look: the one that said the people did not count, that they were just numbers. Georg found, to his horror, that he began to feel the same way. Days were numbers, people were numbers, and even the times he dropped to the gravel or dirt and sought cover were numbers – countless numbers, but they still were numbers he hated. If he thought of anything else, he cannot recall now, except that one day it ended.

It was not so much the date, as the event that sticks in his mind. The war was over, and it was the Yugoslavians and Russians who were ordering the remaining survivors of the siege of Budapest onto trains. His gun was taken away, and he stepped into a dark, overheated prison. He did not know where he was going. He refused to think of his options because there were none. Thinking meant he would fear the known destination: a Russian prison camp. There was no escape. Nobody who went there came back as a whole man, or in some cases even came back alive.

He heard rumors that many of the men from the Russian front who surrendered were now dead. He believed those rumors and decided that he would find a way to live. He owed his family that much. He did not want to be buried in mass unmarked grave somewhere in Russia[71]. He let his mind wander, and he recalls that it was the most hopeless moment of his entire life. He knew no one, and no one would care.

He began to look around his dark confines. He was seated next to a Romanian soldier who was also in the siege of Budapest. They conversed quietly. To his amazement, the Romanian soldier was going to a Romanian camp. Because Georg had learned to speak Romanian in school, he and the soldier were able to understand one another. The soldier told him that if he could prove he was born in Romania, then the guards might drop him off at the Romanian border, too. He recalls the sense of relief when he knew he could say he was born in Romania. However, there was one problem: he did not have his birth certificate anywhere near the train, and he needed it immediately.

The Romanian soldier, whom he learned was from Transylvania as well, promised that he would tell the Russian soldiers when he got off that Georg was of Romanian birth; the rest would be up to him. Georg agreed. He recalls feeling that to ask anything more from this new friend would be too much, and that the Romanian was risking his own life to save his. He had stopped praying a long time before, but now he wanted to begin again.

The train wound its way through the mountainous regions which signaled to Georg that he would soon be in Transylvania. The sounds of his freedom were slowly working their way into his imagination but he dared not say anything. To the amazement and fear of many, especially the Romanian prisoners, the train kept moving. Some argued that they were allies to the Russian Army, as Romania had switched sides at the end of the war, and they begged to be let out, but to no avail. The train chugged eastward.

Georg awoke when the train car lurched to a halt and Russian soldiers ordered everyone out. Blinking in the sunlight, Georg saw some familiar territory; they were still in Romania. He looked at his companion, who was escorted quickly out from the train and then he waited. The train did not move, and the heat was oppressive. He wanted to run, but knew that if he tried to escape, he would be shot. He did not want to be a fool; injured or dead, it would be worse to be injured in the labor camps.

The door opened again, and Georg blinked, and then he heard his name. The Russian soldier was speaking to him, and it took him a moment to realize that he was speaking in Romanian. It was a test. He responded in Romanian, and he was hauled out of the train car by two soldiers. Once he was standing and facing the commander, he was told he would be going to a Romanian prisoner-of-war camp until the matter of his citizenship was sorted out. Georg decided that to answer in anything other than Romanian might send him right in to the heart of Russia. He answered affirmatively: He would accept their decision.

He was sent to the nearest prisoner-of-war camp, and to his dismay, he found out that his family had left Oberneudorf with the rest of the Saxons from all over Northern Transylvania. He was relieved that they were safe and he wondered when and where he might see them again. A short time later, he received word that his family had returned to their village, unlike many other families that he knew. Eventually, he was allowed to leave and make his way on foot to Oberneudorf. He departed as quickly as he could, and he recalls that he nearly sprinted once he was out of sight of the camp. He did not want to think of the barbed wire and the faces of despair ever again. He needed to go home, and he wanted to see his father.

Once he arrived back in Oberneudorf, he saw how much things had changed. His family no longer owned anything. The house his father once owned was now the property of one of the Romanian peasants. His grandfather explained that he now rented that house; he was a tenant and that he worked the land he had once owned for pay. He recalls that the despair in his grandfather's eyes was similar to that of the prisoners of war; a living death. Georg realized that he had nothing in Oberneudorf. The Romanians, he recalls, did give him work but at a low wage. He knew he was unwanted by the Romanians who now owned his land, and they would only appreciate that he was strong and did not cause a fuss. He knew he needed to leave.

After a few years, he moved to Bistritz. He told his sister Maria that it was because in Bistritz, few people would care if he was a German or not, as long as he could work. He realized he could make more money there. He worked for many years as a laborer and found that he earned more money than he needed, so he began to save the extra. He had heard that the communist government of Romania was willing to let the Saxons and other German speaking people immigrate to Germany. With little chance here to make any more money, and no wife or family to worry about, he chose to leave Romania in the early 1960s.

Although his sister moved from Romania to Canada a few years earlier, he decided that Germany would be his destination because he had family there as well. He was nearing his mid forties and he did not want to learn another language, and the prospect of working in a factory did not appeal to him very much. He applied to go to Germany, and he left when he received his immigration papers.

He recalls that, at that time, Germany was still divided between East and West, and he feared that he might somehow arrive on the eastern side of Germany by mistake. The people had fewer freedoms there under the strong communist government that still relied on Russia for financial support. He recalls that his experiences of the war caused his fear, but it was unlikely that he would arrive in the wrong place because it was the West German Government that was allowing him to immigrate within their borders. He gathered his courage and left. He got there, safe and sound, to a place that many Saxons settled and tried to continue on with their lives.

Shortly after he arrived, he bought a new motorcycle. His father had remarried and they had another son. Georg loved the fact that both of them enjoyed riding their motorcycles, and it gave Georg a good opportunity to spend time and get to know his younger half-brother. The one thing he did not like was the fact that his brother was rash on the bike and enjoyed driving it fast, perhaps a bit too fast, and he worried that something might happen to him.

However, Georg had other things to worry about. He had a new job, and he went there each day early in the morning. His brother would return home after his own work day finished late in the evening. One evening he didn't return. Georg was worried, but not too much. He believed his brother had stayed late at his job because he often accepted extra shifts. With that in mind, he took his own motorcycle and set out to work the next morning.

Traffic was slow that day. There was not usually too much that early in the morning, but sometimes there was an accident. This was not out of the ordinary, for in those days there were often breakdowns or small accidents or cars in ditches with people waiting by the side of the road for someone to help them.

He stopped his motorcycle close to the scene of the accident because he was curious. As he normally did, he looked to see what sorts of cars were involved, but this time he saw it was a motorcycle. He looked closer, and to his horror, he saw that the motorcycle was the same model as the one his brother drove. He recalls the feeling of cold sweat and his racing heart as he moved closer to inspect the crash site. His voice sounded old beyond his years when he asked if there was anything he could do to help.

On a grassy knoll, he saw the motorcycle victim. He shuddered at the thought of another death in front of him. He walked closer, hoping to find a way to help, instinctively trying to do something. As he drew closer, he could begin to make out the face of the young man on the ground. The face looked familiar, and at first, Georg did not believe that it could be *him*. Georg began to cry. He had never cried in his entire life – not in Budapest, not even in the train – but here, by the body of his young brother, he cried. Budapest and certain death was bad, and heading to Russia was worse, but this was sheer pain. He believed that he had encouraged his younger brother to ride the motorcycle that caused his untimely death. Georg wanted to be angry at anyone but himself, but he knew that his brother would be alive if he hadn't been on that machine.

Georg vowed that he would never ride any motorcycle ever again. True to his word, that evening he posted a "for sale" sign on his motorcycle and received good money for it, but that did not help with the feelings of despair. Georg recalls that he gladly would have paid all the money he had to see his brother alive again. Still, despite this horrible event, his life continued on the course that he planned. He misses his brother dearly, though; he always will.

He was pleased by many events he saw come to pass in Germany, in particular the fall of the Berlin Wall and the formation of a new, unified Germany; and a more peaceful one at that. He recalls that, in a way, by living his life in Germany, he had the chance to see the rebirth of Europe firsthand. He does not follow politics, but he wonders why people are getting as nationalistic as they are. He says he does not worry about another war – there are too many checks and balances in place, for now at least. He does not want to think about what might happen 10 years from now. He believes that if the checks and balances are removed or are made irrelevant… but he stops himself from finishing this thought and says that the subsequent war would be far worse than anyone could possibly imagine.

His memories still haunt him, although in later years, he feels that by living in Germany it has allowed him to come to terms with his past. He enjoys the infrequent visits from his nephew and nieces and their families from Canada. They are far away, and yet, by picking up the phone and writing letters, he knows that he can enjoy their company. His great-nieces are older, with children of their own, and he hopes that they will pass on his knowledge. It would be wonderful if they pass on the traditions of the Saxons, or a small part of their history. However, he comments that this is his sister's concern. There are benefits to being a great-great-uncle: He has less responsibility this way. He fears that he was irresponsible once, and he does not want this to happen again.

Nearly 85 now, he finds it a bit harder to go on his much-cherished walks, but good people still fill his life. His cousin chuckles and comments that life is still pretty good for him. Georg still doesn't say much to anyone.

Georg laughs, saying he is only telling me the important things. That is the way it should be. In his defence he asks me, did he tell me all of the important things? I tell him no, because there is still so much of his life he needs to live.

Notes

1 Ernst Wagner mentions these numbers in the book The Transylvanian Saxons, and he believes that closer to 2,000 people than to 20,000 people moved to Transylvania at that time.

2 Wagner takes pains to point out that this idyllic story is part of the lore and traditions that the Saxons hold dear. The Saxons were invited to protect a supposedly sparsely populated land, but in fact, there were already Hungarians and Romanians on that land who would not swear loyalty to the crown.

3 Magyarization was the process by which the Hungarian government encouraged the Romanians and Germans in the Kingdom Hungary to adopt the local culture, specifically by adopting the Hungarian language and the Roman Catholic faith practices.

4 According to The Compact Timeline of World War II, the ethnic Romanians were given 14 days to leave Hungarian-controlled Northern Transylvania and settle in the south.

5 This is mentioned in several books: Inschert, Wagner, Böhm and Csallner.

6 This was common within many countries of Europe at this time, and is common today in some, where some sort of military service is mandatory.

7 In 1930, the population of Bistritz was about 30,000 and the entire Saxon population in Romania was approximately

746,000 people. Comparatively, Heidendorf's population was about 650.

8 Most weddings were held in the wintertime after a short engagement because there was less daily work for the villagers to do.

9 Children born even a month early were a concern in this time because the lack of modern medical knowledge, or money to pay a doctor's fees, meant that they could not do much for a premature baby who could not thrive on its own.

10 The Sudetenland was part of Czechoslovakia and it was home to ethnic Germans. The Munich agreement was made on 29 September 1938 to appease Nazi Germany.

11 The Munich Agreement between Great Britain and Germany gave Europe peace for less than one year.

12 The Great War (1914-1918) began when Imperial Germany invaded the neutrality of Belgium, and Great Britain, a guarantor of the neutrality of Belgium, stood up to defend them.

13 Typhoid was often fatal in those days, and although most people did not understand what caused the disease, many understood it was connected to poor quality water and sanitation. Although there was a vaccine, it was often too costly for many people.

14 They were ordered to evacuate due to the retreat of the German soldiers before the Russian lines advanced through Transylvania. Since the Saxons were of Germanic origin, if they were captured, they would likely face deportation to Russia. This was the fate of many Saxons who still resided in Southern Transylvania.

15 This is a small village found in Northern Transylvania, a population of about 600 people. It still stands today but it is now a part of the larger city of Bistriţa, Romania.

16 This was common and the people I interviewed emphasized the importance of the local midwife. Having a doctor

present at a birth meant that it would be dangerous indeed. Most times, even if there was a threat to the life of the mother or child, there was no money to pay the doctor to be present.

17 Since 1919, when Hungary ceded Transylvania to Romania, school children of all ethnic backgrounds were required to learn Romanian, this included Hungarian and German children.

18 After the Treaty of Trianon in 1920, which transferred Transylvania to Romania, policy changed.

19 The same assimilation process took place under Hungarian rule, when the government forced the Romanian nobility and others to learn Hungarian and to convert to the Roman Catholic Church. This was called Magyarization.

20 Now diphtheria is preventable with a vaccine and treatable with an antitoxin and antibiotics, but in that time most victims who were young or were already weak succumbed to it. It is a bacterial disease that is contagious when left untreated, and those who have survived the disease can contract it again.

21 The Saxons had not lived within the Borders of Germany for centuries but they were called the Volksdeutsche by Hitler. He believed that even though they still had few ties to Germany now, they would still support their fellow Germans in this cause.

22 According to Evan and Gibbons, Hitler aimed to unite Austria and Germany. The record shows that the citizens voted overwhelmingly in favour of uniting the two countries. However, if one examines the situation more closely, one sees that the voting was not done in secret, and on the voting card, the circle for voting "Ja" was large and in the centre and the circle for "Nein" was small and set off to the right. Mazower concludes that people's votes were motivated by fear.

23 This was known as the Vienna Awards, and it was the second of these Awards which arbitrarily granted the Northern part of Transylvania to Hungary. This was voted on by two judges from Germany and Italy.

24 His mother was the famous Queen Marie of Romania who died in 1938. Carol wanted to develop a cult of personality, possibly in an effort to not be overshadowed by his politicians.

25 This was the official beginning of the Second World War, between Germany and Poland, and although hailed as a German victory, the war itself lasted for seven weeks.

26 A grandchild of Queen Marie of Romania, he became King in 1934 at age eleven, and his uncle Paul was regent prince until he came of age. Once King Peter assumed power at age seventeen, he began to withdraw the support his uncle had for Hitler.

27 These were primarily members of the Nazi Youth party, who were sent out to countries which had a high number of Volksdeutsche in the population. Hitler believed that if lands they lived in became a part of Greater Germany, the people would be more willing to support his philosophy and follow the orders of the Third Reich.

28 Often, the younger men were promised money, education, or better working conditions in exchange for signing to support the German Army. Some were promised that even if they signed up they would not be sent away, they would only be asked to visibly support the Germans within the villages. This was a first step to getting them to fight. If polite bribes did not work, then the threats of harm to the men and their loved ones began, and later escalated.

29 Snipers often lay in wait to shoot at the men as they disembarked from the trains.

30 Many men of German origin from other parts of Europe who were too old for active military service in Russia and elsewhere, and who needed money, went to Berlin to work.

There were rumours that the sons of men who chose to work in Berlin were not sent to the front lines, but this was only hearsay.

31　By this time, Yugoslavian guerrilla warriors rebelled against the Nazi occupation of the country.

32　The Saxons were not the only ethnic Germans in Transylvania. Banat and Sathmar Swabians, Besarabia, Dobrudja and Bukovina Germans, and people from other parts of Germany and Austria had also immigrated and settled there.

33　By the end of the war, Northern Transylvania was returned to Romania. This was because Romania argued at the Paris Peace Talks of 1945 that they were allies with Great Britain and France, and that the Vienna Awards were invalid. Since Hungary was a part of the losing side, and was also under Soviet Influence, the allies agreed with Romania's argument.

34　Many of the villages suffered losses in the First World War in the Austrian Imperial Army, and these are listed in the villages' books and elsewhere.

35　Peter's siblings tell me that their parents and elder siblings talked about this lost sister, but Michael did not talk too much about her.

36　Comparisons were often made between children in a family, and the quieter children were often praised and the more active children were encouraged to emulate the quiet ones.

37　Most children did not have any specific responsibilities related to the church service. This changed once they were confirmed, often at the age of thirteen or fourteen. The confirmation service took place in the spring, usually before Easter.

38　Budapest was home to a well-respected agricultural school, and many Saxons studied there to learn how to improve their farming techniques.

39　Most of the people whose lands were in the South or farther East of Germany meant something different when they said "Eastern Front." Generally, they are referring to Russia,

Finland, Yugoslavia. The Saxons refer to France and Italy as the Western Front.

40 There was a cavalry division with a large number of Saxons in it that suffered significant losses in the siege of Budapest. Michael might have possibly been in this one, but his siblings are unable to confirm this fact.

41 Many countries chose to rewrite their history to reflect their people positively. For example, Romanians taught their children that victories in the Great War (WWI) were rewarded so they received the land they did. In reality, these lands were granted by way of a peace treaty in 1919. Most of the resources of the Transylvanian Saxons mention this as well.

42 Transylvania was given to Romania along to with other territory from other defeated countries by way of the Treaty of Trianon and the Treaty of Paris. However it should be noted that Besserabia, which was then a part of Soviet Russia, was not returned to Romania.

43 Many people I interviewed talked about men from Germany's Nazi party coming to their villages and interviewing the men and older boys; it seems that there was a push to bring the Volksdeutsche more into line with the German Reich.

44 This was a result of the Second Vienna Awards. Further information can be found in Foisel and Wagner.

45 By this time, the German monarchy was in exile, and even though many of the German aristocracy supported Hitler, he already was moving against them. This was in an effort to push for his own cult of personality.

46 Many of these men recall that winters in the years 1940 through 1942 were some of the coldest in the area living memory. This is supported many of the books that confirm that the these were some of the coldest winters on record in Europe.

47 When the United States of America joined the fighting in the final years of World War I, the German and Austrian Empire began to lose ground.

48 As the war losses began to mount, most people and books report that the army began to recruit and train young boys to fight.

49 Many men would not learn about the Nazi death camps until later, but it was common knowledge that there were many unpleasant places that people would be sent to work, and they were often referred to as labour camps. The Saxons would not find out the full horror of the camps until they arrived in Germany after they were evacuated.

50 The Saxons did not benefit in the way many had anticipated, and it was the Hungarians who received a small amount of additional land and slightly lowered taxes as an appeasing gesture by Romania.

51 Many of the younger men recall that they found out information by overhearing conversations, and much was not told to them directly.

52 The men I spoke with made it clear that these groups were there long before the Nazis entered the villages, and even the smaller villages books bear this information out. Dr Dietmar Plajer believes that these interesting and educational orders were created by the Saxons to foster a sense of fellowship among the youth and were founded on the principals of the Church and reflected God's commandments.

53 The Saxons were Volksdeutsch, which means that they were ethnic German people living outside of German territory. In his grand design, Hitler viewed the Volksdeutsch as less important than those who lived within the Greater German borders.

54 Based upon comments and books, many people felt that there would be a repeat of The First world War when the German armies defeated the Russian armies and took much of the land from Russia after the 1917 Russian revolution.

55 Austria was still a part of Greater Germany at this point, but many recall that the Saxons still referred to that specific area as Austria.

56 Churches and family members in Canada would sponsor people to come to Canada, and once they arrived, the Saxons often worked as field and farm labourers to pay back the immigration fees.

57 Typhoid was a constant threat to health in many of the Saxon villages. Community creaks and wells were often a source of contagion. If a family had a separate source of water, they were less likely to fall ill.

58 The invasion of Poland by Germany marked the start of the war. This battle was over in seven weeks, and most in Europe believed that it would not affect them in any major way. This was followed shortly by the seven-month-long Sitzkrieg (a play on the word Blitzkrieg) where both sides were encamped but did not fight, and then the war began in earnest in May 1940 with the Battle of France.

59 In predominantly Saxon villages in Northern Transylvania, not much changed. Some of my interview subjects recalled that the few Romanians who lived in their villages left for the south, and Hungarians moved into those homes.

60 Almost anyone who seemed to be younger than 45 was "asked" to go to Russia or one of the other fighting fronts.

61 Most of the villages heard the order to evacuate from the village radio although some received it from a messenger on horseback, but people seemed to suspect for some time that there would be some news because evacuation plans had already been prepared by Northern Transylvania's regional officials.

62 At the end of the war many of the Saxons travelled to Germany in search of a better life. They settled in groups in many southern German cities.

63 By looking at older maps and plotting the landmarks past which the boys walked, I infer that this camp was in eastern Czechoslovakia, close to the border with Transylvania.

64 The Nazis promised people many things, but most of the men recall that the Nazis stirred up emotions of loss within the villagers and promoted the benefits of a return to power. Many books and documents bear this out.

65 In many villages, children began attending school at the age of six, and Böhm makes a point of writing this in her book.

66 The First Vienna Award transferred lands from Czechoslovakia to Hungary, and the Second Vienna Award split Transylvania between Hungary and Romania.

67 Elections were seldom contested, and most candidates were nominated and acclaimed.

68 There was always talk of the war going badly but the officials on the radio emphasized smaller victories and spoke little of the defeats.

69 Many men would make comments to this effect that they felt that the Nazi party members chose to come to the villages to avoid direct combat action in Russia or on other fronts.

70 Hitler directly ordered these commanders to hold Buda and Pest, and not to surrender or retreat.

71 Most of the prisoners of war from the siege of Budapest died in Russia. The information that the men were alive was proven incorrect after the Nuremberg trials.

Bibliography

Interviews:

Emrich, Anna, Personal Interview, Rebecca A. Emrich, June 2007

Emrich, Anna, Telephone Interview, Rebecca A. Emrich, July 2008

Emrich, Anna, Telephone Interview, Rebecca A. Emrich, September, 2008

Emrich, Anna, Personal Interview, Rebecca A. Emrich, June 2008

Emrich, Dieter, Telephone Interview, Rebecca A. Emrich, June 2008

Emrich, John, Telephone Interview, Rebecca A. Emrich, July 2008

Emrich, Rose Marie, Telephone Interview, Rebecca A. Emrich, June 2008

Emrich, John, Personal Interview, Rebecca A. Emrich, July 2009

Emrich, Johann, Personal Interview, Rebecca A. Emrich, July 2009

Emrich, Johann, Telephone Interview, Rebecca A. Emrich, September, 2008

Emrich, Johann, Telephone Interview, Rebecca A. Emrich, November, 2008

Emrich, Michael, Personal Interview, Rebecca A. Emrich, September, 2008

Emrich, Rosina, Personal Interview, Rebecca A. Emrich, September, 2008

Eichvald, Anna, Personal Interview, Rebecca A. Emrich, June, 2008

Gross, Georg, Telephone Interview, Conversation with Rosina Emrich, September, 2008

German Consulate, Email, Rebecca A. Emrich August, 2008

German Consulate, Phone Conversation, Rebecca A. Emrich, September, 2008

Intschert, Michael, Telephone Interview, Rebecca A. Emrich, August, 2008

Intschert, Michael, Telephone Interview, Rebecca A. Emrich, October, 2008

Hanek, Michael, Personal Interview, Rebecca A. Emrich, July, 2008

Hanek, Katharina, Personal Interview, Rebecca A. Emrich, July, 2008

Hanek, Katharina, Telephone Interview, Rebecca A, Emrich, September, 2009

Hendel, John, Personal Interview, Rebecca A. Emrich, July, 2008

Hendel, John, Telephone Interview, Rebecca A. Emrich, September, 2009

Hendel, Sophia, Personal Interview, Rebecca A. Emrich, July, 2008

Penteker, John, Personal Interview, Rebecca A. Emrich, June, 2008

Penteker, John, Telephone Interview, Rebecca A. Emrich, August 2008

Penteker, Judy, Telephone Interview, Rebecca A. Emrich, August, 2008

Romanian Consulate, Email, Rebecca A. Emrich, October, 2008

Scholtes, Waldemar, Telephone Interview, Rebecca A. Emrich, October, 2009

Scholtes, Waldemar, Personal Interview, Rebecca A. Emrich, October, 2009

Tinnes, Maria, Personal Interview, Rebecca A. Emrich, August, 2008

Tinnes, Maria, Telephone Interview, Rebecca A. Emrich, October, 2008

Wilging, Maria, Telephone Interview, Rebecca A. Emrich, September, 2008

Wilging, Maria, Telephone Interview, Rebecca A. Emrich, November, 2008

Books and Other Sources:

These are books and other documents, which the author has either referred to in this book or used to confirm details given by the interviews.

Böhm, Maria. Mein Heimatort Oberneudorf: Die Geschichte Der Oberneudorfer Sachsen Im Nösnergau In Nordsiebenburgen Rumanien. Mellrichstadt: 1991

Cawthorne, Nigel. Battles of WWII: an Illustrated Account of the Major Campaigns, From Europe to the Pacific Islands. London: Arcturus Publishing, 2003

Cawthorne. Nigel. 100 Tyrants: History's Most Evil; Despots & Dictators. London: Arcturus Publishing Limited, 2008

Csallner, Kurt. Heidendorfer Heimatbuch. Hilfskomitee der Siebenbürger Sachsen. 1969

Darman, Peter. World War II Trivia Book, London: Brown Reference Book, 2007

Evans, A.A. and Gibbons, David. The Compact Timeline of World War II, Herdforthshire: Worth Press Ltd., 2008

Foisel, John. Saxons Through Seventeen Centuries: A History of the Transylvanian Saxons. Cleveland, Ohio: Central Publishing House, 1936

Green, Lowell C. Lutherans Against Hitler: the Untold Story. St. Louis: Concordia Publishing House, 2007

Intscher, Martin et al. Transylvanian Saxons. Cleveland: The Alliance of Transylvanian Saxons, 1982

Intschert, Michael translated by Judy Penteker. <u>My Memoirs.</u> Kitchener: Self-published, 2007

Mazower, Mark. <u>Hitler's Empire: How the Nazis Ruled Europe</u>. New York: Penguin Press, 2008

Messanger, Charles. <u>Wars That Changed The World: The Defining Conflicts of World History From The Ancient Greeks To The War On Terror</u>. London: Quercus Publishing Plc, 2008

Nagorski, Andrew. <u>The Greatest Battle: Stalin, Hitler, and the Desperate Struggle for Moscow that Changed the Course of World War II</u>, New York: Simon & Schuster Paperbacks, 2007

Riley, Bronwen. <u>Transylvania</u>. London: Frances Lincoln, 2007

Süssmuth, Rita, Editor. <u>Fragen an die Deutsche Geschichtes; Ideen, Kräfte, Entscheidungen von 1800 bis zur Gegenwart English Edition</u>. Bonn: German Budestag Publications Section, 1993

Wagner, Margaret E. Et al. <u>The Library of Congress World War II Companion</u>. New York: Simon and Shuster, 2007

Weinberg, Gerhard. <u>Visions of Victory: The Hopes of Eight World War II Leaders</u>, New York: Cambridge University Press, 2005

Zillich, Henrich. <u>Siebenbürgen Ein Abendländisches Schicksal</u>. Stuttgart: Karl Robert Langewiesche, 1957

Made in the USA
Charleston, SC
26 November 2011